GROWING UP IN GRACE

The Use of Means for
Communion with God

GROWING UP IN GRACE

The Use of Means for
Communion with God

MURRAY G. BRETT

REFORMATION HERITAGE BOOKS
Grand Rapids, Michigan

REFORMATION HERITAGE BOOKS
2965 Leonard St., NE
Grand Rapids, MI 49525
616-977-0599 / Fax 616-285-3246
e-mail: orders@heritagebooks.org
website: www.heritagebooks.org

Library of Congress Cataloging-in-Publication Data

Brett, Murray G., 1960-
  Growing up in grace : the use of means for communion with
God / Murray G. Brett.
    p. cm.
  Includes bibliographical references.
  ISBN 978-1-60178-061-4 (pbk. : alk. paper)
  1. Spiritual life--Reformed Baptists. 2. Repentance--Reformed
Baptists. 3. Grace (Theology) I. Title.
  BV4501.3.B7475 2009
  248.4--dc22
                                         2009008407

---

*For additional Reformed literature, both new and used,
request a free book list from the above address.*

In memory of Dada, my paternal grandfather, from whom I first learned to love the Word of God, and of Granny Brett, whose persevering, reverent trust in Christ I still draw upon...

In memory of Big Murray, my maternal grandfather, from whom I learned to work hard for my dreams, and in memory of Granny Hazel, who passed on to me the love of learning...

To my father, Lintorn, who gives boundlessly, and to my mother, Willoise, who serves tirelessly, from whom I hope to learn to give and serve just a fraction as much as they have...

To my father- and mother-in-law, Paul and Irene Rowell, who gave me the greatest earthly treasure I have—my wife...

To my three sons,

Nathan, whose prayers and resolve to live a holy life have paid dividends for both of us...

Benjamin, whose amiable, diligent spirit encourages me to persevere in doing good...

Ethan, whose determination inspires me to be a more steadfast man...

To my daughter, Bethany Eileen, who was the first one in our family born during a hard, four-year trek through seminary and whose names mean "light in the house of poverty." Thank you so much for bringing light and music into my life and our home.

Finally to my wife, Paula, my love and constant companion. No man ever had a more suitable companion for the work of the Christian ministry.

Special Thanks

————— ❦ —————

I would like to say how much I appreciate the friends who encouraged me along the way and others who took time to read and offer suggestions to improve the clarity and usefulness of the book. Wayne Roper's encouragement, keen insight, and friendship are all of incalculable value to me. From the very beginning, in planting the church here in Commerce and in my writing, you have been and continue to be a cherished friend. As a young pastor, I used to be able to say that pastor Steve Martin gave me all the best books in my library. Now after nearly thirteen years of having known Steve, I can only say that he has recommended the best books for my library because I bought nearly all that he's suggested and a few more besides. Also, I am very grateful, my brother, for the "big picture" comments you offered for improving the book. In addition, I am deeply indebted to pastor Geoffrey Thomas. I have perhaps learned as much from Geoff as from John Bunyan and D. Martyn Lloyd-Jones as to how to preach to and shepherd the heart. Experimental (experiential) Calvinism seems far too rare in our day, and faithful experimental preaching seems even more rare. I hope to continue to grow under your example, my dear friend. I would also like to offer a special word of thanks to Mrs. Anna Maupin who gave the first serious editorial help and then to Mrs. Delia Mixon who read, read, and re-read with a fine-tooth comb. Many, many thanks as well to Jay Collier of Reformation Heritage Books for shepherding this book through the process. You are a gracious brother. Thank you all!

Contents

Foreword

Murray Brett's book is an exhortation to the full-orbed discipleship of the Lord Jesus Christ. He is pleading for experiential Calvinistic living, a translation into daily Christian service of lives lived under that vision of the world in which God is adored as the sovereign Creator and Sustainer of the universe, the One who in His immeasurable love has provided His own Son to be the Savior of the world, who by His royal death has accomplished a cosmic redemption which God applies to favored sinners by the Holy Spirit commissioned by Jesus Christ.

The coming of the Spirit to the sinner convicts of sin, illuminates, makes discovery of the beauty of Christ, and knits the heart to the Lord for a life of service. Such a divine work cannot but create such spiritual fruit as love, joy, and peace, a hunger for righteousness, a readiness to turn the other cheek, and a willingness to forgive seventy times seven. A call to such godliness is the theme of this book and it is written in essentially experiential terms. In other words, Murray's concern is not that there is a change in theological convictions—there is no doubt that he is pleading for that—but he longs for something more from his readers, a change in heart attitude, in stronger affection for God and for our neighbors so that through love our lives will count for Christ.

The book is a plea that we do the will of God. Isn't that the sum of the Christian life? If we had gone to Joseph's carpenter's shop in Nazareth and asked the young man working for His father what He was doing as He fashioned some piece of furniture, He would reply, "The will of God." If we had met Him in Galilee some years later and seen Him giving sight to the blind and cleansing to the leper, and heard one of His sermons and asked Him what He was doing, "The will of God," He would have replied. If at the end of His life we had ascended Golgotha and approached Him in His agony on the cross and had asked, "Son of God, what are you doing?" He might again have answered, "The will of God." The will of God was the only thing that He ever did, and it is the only thing we must do.

What is the significance of that? It is that true piety does not feed on experience. Godliness feeds on Christ, on His truth, on the mysteries of God's revelation, and on His promises which are all yea and amen in Christ. Murray's book is helpful because it recoils from the experientialism which makes human experience the center of interest and preoccupation. Let us learn of the Jesus whom our souls love. Let us grow closer to Him each day.

Christianity as possession is not simply an experience of salvation in the past, nor simply a status once for all bestowed. It is a high and holy vocation to be fulfilled in all who name Christ's name. We dare not rest until we attain to the prize of the high calling of God in Christ Jesus.

This book addresses our consciences about the character of our Christian way. Is there credible godliness? Is there a deepening, growing relationship with our Lord? Is the love of Jesus Christ constraining our behavior—love so amazing, so divine demanding our souls, our lives, and our all—and are we giving the Lord affectionate obedience in return? That is the formidable challenge of Murray's book. We long for it to be the first of many to come from his pen. The world is richer for this legacy from Georgia, the lovely lines, the sweetening influence, the signposts all pointing to the Savior.

Geoff Thomas
Alfred Place Baptist Church, Aberystwyth, Wales

Introduction

How be ya gonna find the treasure wi'out the map?

"THE BLACK SPOT! Well, shiver me timber," says Silver. "What be this? This here was cut from a Bible! What fool's cut a Bible? Was it you, Job Andersen? Now Job can say his prayers. He's had his slice a luck, Job has. Cut a Bible.... You'll all swing now!"

"Belay that talk, John Silver. This crew has tipped you the spot in full counsel. The rules is, you turn it over to see duty bound what's wrote there," snarls George Merry.

"Thank ye, George, you always was braced for business," Long John replies. Silver turns the page over and says, "'Deposed!' And very pretty wrote...."

George Merry growls, "You can't fool this crew no more, John Silver. Step down off your perch and vote."

In the background, a voice calls to Silver. It's the voice of the good doctor come to inquire about young Jim Hawkins, and Silver turns to say to the pirates, "There'll be no vot'n 'til the business of this here map be disposed of. 'Til then I'm still cap'n and your black spot ain't worth a biscuit."

George Merry answers, "Map or no map, we ain't giv'n up no 'ostage until we lays eyes on the treasure itself. Am I right, mates?" And all the pirates howl approvingly, "Harrr, Harrr."

Then aptly Long John Silver replies, *"How be ya gonna find the treasure wi'out the map?"*

Long John and Jim go together and meet the doctor, and the doctor tends young Jim's knife wound. Slyly, Silver lets Jim and the doctor know that he is now in possession of the map and bargains for his life. Silver and Jim return to the front of the Fort and Silver throws the map down on the ground. The pirates cheer. Then John Silver holds up the piece of paper with the black spot on it. Another pirate urges George Merry to take it back and tear it up. But Silver, holding onto the paper, glares at the pirates and says, "Put 'em back in the Good Book, mate. Poor rov'n seamen the likes a' you needs every scrap of Scripture he can get!"

There's a "scrap of Scripture" in Isaiah 25:6 which likens the glories of the gospel to the richest food and finest wine, and a scrap in Job 22:21–26 which likens God the Father to the purest gold. There's another scrap in Matthew 13:45–46 which likens Jesus to a pearl of greatest price. John 14:16 likens the Holy Spirit to a Comforter who draws us away from the spirit of orphans into a spirit of sonship. And Long John Silver was right—*you simply can't find these treasures without the map!* The map is the only means appointed by God to find the treasure.

In John 5:39, Jesus told the religious people of His day that they searched the Scriptures because they believe that in them they possess eternal life. But Jesus said, "The Scriptures testify of me" (John 5:39). Studying sacred Scripture is not an end in itself. It is a means to an end, and that end is *communion with our great Triune God*. My aim is to help you make use of what a former, very spiritually minded generation of believers called "the means of grace." We simply cannot grow in the experience of grace without the right understanding and right use of the means. An old pastor named John Blair wrote that many passages represent God's Word and His ordinances as means of quickening, supporting, comforting, sanctifying, perfecting, and strengthening God's people. These means of grace do not have intrinsic value in themselves. They are not rendered effectual by any power or will in us, but they are rendered effectual and attain their appointed end by the blessing of the Holy Spirit upon them and by His energy in them. So while God commands us to use these means, they are truly means in the Holy Spirit's hands, rather than in ours.[1]

One of the means which God appointed to accomplish His purposes in the lives of His people is the devotional study of His holy Word. "How be ya gonna find the treasure wi'out the map?" You cannot! Sacred Scripture gives us the only Christ whom we may know. Yet, however faithful and purposeful, Bible study is not the only means which God has appointed to get to know, love, obey, and worship Him. He uses other means of grace and growth as well: prayer, confession, repentance, self-denial, praise, reproof, correction, the sacraments, and the corporate life and witness of the local church. God employs all these to further our growth in grace and in fulfilling our chief end: to glorify God and enjoy Him forever. Growth is never automatic and the use of means is never mechanical as if we were plugging numbers into a math formula or a calculator and out pops the solution. We must combine the use of the means of grace with faith. Christian growth requires dependence

---

1. John Blair, "An Essay on the Means of Grace," *Sermons of the Log College* (Ligonier: Soli Deo Gloria, 1993), 209.

upon God's Spirit, not mere dependence upon principles or steps, whether there are twelve or twelve hundred.

Growing Up is not intended to be an exhaustive study of the private or public means of grace in order to live a Godward life. Rather, it is a sort of manual exemplifying the use of means to grow in grace with a handful of guides to encourage faithful, daily, experiential Christianity. It is my earnest prayer that this book will help you better learn to make use of every means God has appointed so that together we all might *Grow Up in Grace* for the sake of the glory of God and for our and others' greatest good.

DISCUSS THE ISSUES

1. Define the term "means of grace" and give examples. What is the purpose of the means of grace?

2. What happened to the people in Jesus' day who "searched the Scriptures" without ever having their hearts turned towards Christ (John 5:39)? What will happen to us if we use the means of grace as an end in themselves?

3. What causes "the means of grace" to be effective in our lives in attaining God's appointed ends? How may we keep "the means of grace" from becoming mechanical? Why is Christian growth never to be seen as a matter of merely following principles?

4. Do you agree or disagree that the Bible gives us the only Christ whom we may know? Explain your answer. Read Job

22:21–26, Matthew 13:45–46, and John 14:15–21. What are the means and the ends in each of these passages?

SOLVE THE SCENARIO

Mike and Sandy have been dating for about four months and Mike would like to see their relationship deepen. Mike is a cool guy and Sandy really likes him, but she's expressed her concern to him about his lack of spiritual leadership. His initial response seemed good, and he seems to want to grow as a Christian and as a leader, but it's too early for Sandy to tell if he really takes his relationship with Christ and his role as a spiritual leader seriously. Both were raised in Christian homes, both profess faith in Christ, and both are members of a local church, though not the same church. Mike's church is evangelical, but it doesn't take doctrine very seriously and tends to be more moralistic in practice. Sandy's church seeks to keep the gospel central for the whole of the Christian life and for the life of the church and, though they take doctrine seriously, they are very warm-hearted and experiential. Mike's family never practiced family worship while he was growing up and even now Mike reads the Bible devotionally only occasionally. He skips church on Sunday about once a month during the summer to go to the lake skiing with his buddies. He asked Sandy to drive up to the lake with him next Sunday morning and go skiing for the day.

What would you counsel Sandy to do about missing church to go with Mike and why? If Mike is serious about growing as a Christian, what would you tell him to do and why?

SIT AT THE FEET OF CHRIST-CENTERED, EXPERIENTIAL TEACHERS

The Discipline of Grace, by Jerry Bridges (*Level:* Basic)

Spiritual Disciplines, by Donald S. Whitney (*Level:* Basic), www. mindspring.com/~skazmarek/discplne/index.htm

Follow the Lamb, by Horatius Bonar (*Level:* Basic)

Walking with God, by J. C. Ryle (*Level:* Basic)

Practical Religion, by J. C. Ryle (*Level:* Basic to Intermediate)

Spiritual Disciplines for the Christian Life, by Donald S. Whitney (*Level:* Basic)

"The Happiness of Drawing Near to God," a sermon by Thomas Watson (*Level:* Basic to Intermediate), *www. reformedsermonarchives.com/Wat6.htm*

"Christ To Be Found In the Ordinances, With the Import and Happy Effects of Finding Him," pp. 480–520, volume 10 in "The Works of Thomas Boston," by Thomas Boston (*Level:* Intermediate)

"Prayer as a Means of Grace," in "Faith and Life," by B. B. Warfield (*Level:* Intermediate)

"Meditation a Means of Grace," by Robert L. Dabney, I: 543–653 (*Level:* Intermediate)

Romans 5:1–11

Therefore being justified by faith, we have peace with God through our Lord Jesus Christ: [2]By whom also we have access by faith into this grace wherein we stand, and rejoice in hope of the glory of God. [3]And not only so, but we glory in tribulations also: knowing that tribulation worketh patience; [4]And patience, experience; and experience, hope: [5]And hope maketh not ashamed; because the love of God is shed abroad in our hearts by the Holy Ghost which is given unto us. [6]For when we were yet without strength, in due time Christ died for the ungodly. [7]For scarcely for a righteous man will one die: yet peradventure for a good man some would even dare to die. [8]But God commendeth his love toward us, in that, while we were yet sinners, Christ died for us. [9]Much more then, being now justified by his blood, we shall be saved from wrath through him. [10]For if, when we were enemies, we were reconciled to God by the death of his Son, much more, being reconciled, we shall be saved by his life. [11]And not only so, but we also joy in God through our Lord Jesus Christ, by whom we have now received the atonement.

CHAPTER ONE

Finding Happiness in Communion with God

A LOOK AT THE CHIEF END FROM THE BEGINNING

THE LAST CRUSADE is the grand finale for Indiana Jones. First, the young Indy discovers his life's mission. As the story unfolds, his mission culminates in "the greatest of all searches," the search for the Holy Grail. Some say that the Grail is the cup from which Christ drank at the Last Supper, and to drink from this cup is said to bring eternal youth.

The quest for the "Holy Grail" is *the big one.* We might even call it *the spiritual big one.* It symbolizes our search for significance, our search for ultimate happiness which is far greater than mere eternal youth or immortality. But the path of true significance and real happiness is paved with many pitfalls, perhaps the biggest of which is the lack of an overarching purpose for the whole of life.

Purpose is central in giving meaning to life. It is the glue that causes life to cohere and the motivation that causes us to persevere.

We've all heard it before. A man stands to tell his story in a room packed full of dream chasers. He says, "You know that I've been very fortunate in my career to make a lot of money. I've made far more than I ever dreamed, far more than I could ever spend, and far more than my family needs. To be honest, one of my motives for making so much money was simple. I want to have the money to hire people to do what I don't like doing. But there's one thing I've never been able to hire anyone to do for me and that is to find my own sense of meaning and fulfillment in life, and I'd give anything to discover that."[1]

Thomas Carlyle, the eighteenth-century Scottish satirist, once said that the person without purpose is like a ship without a rudder, a homeless wanderer, a nothing, a no-man. But God gives grace for one purpose, for one central purpose, for one chief end, and it is that He might be worshiped and glorified as God!

FINDING YOUR GREATEST HAPPINESS IN COMMUNION WITH GOD

If you've studied the War Between the States, you will surely know that from Gettysburg to Appomattox was from the pinnacle to the pit for the Confederacy. Most historians portray their demise as a downward spiral from the heights of assurance to the depths of despair. The exultant hopes of a proud and powerful army withered continually until their final surrender.

In Romans 5:1–11, Paul depicts just the opposite. He starts in the depths of despair and rises to the height of assurance and happiness in communion with God. Exultant joy rises higher and higher as we move from being the enemies of God at odds with Him to being in the most

---

1. Os Guinness, *The Call* (Nashville, TN: Word Publishing, 1998), 1.

intimate fellowship of grace and love imaginable. As a result of justification, verse 2 says, "we rejoice in hope of the glory of God." Then verse 3 climbs a little higher than rejoicing in our hope of heaven only. Paul uses a device to mark out the progression of rejoicing for us. His phrase "and not only so" marks the assent upwards. The assurance of God's love for us is so great, we may rejoice not only in our future happiness, "we glory in tribulations also." Then in verse 11, Paul climbs higher still. We may rejoice not only in our present sufferings and the fruit of assurance that these experiences of grace bear in our lives; more than this, we may rejoice in God Himself.

According to Thomas Goodwin, the consummate fruit of justifying grace is communion with God. And that communion is a vital, mind-engaging, heart-affecting, will-moving fellowship. Faith is not an end in itself; instead it is the instrumental means of justifying grace. But justification is not an end in itself either. In Romans 5, Paul regards justification as a means for the privilege of access to God. Then, in Romans 6, he regards justification as one of the primary motives for growth in holiness. But neither is holiness an end in itself. Holiness is the means for making our access to God sweeter and even more enjoyable. So Goodwin concludes that enjoying communion with God is the end of all our graces.[2]

We've been granted the great and glorious privilege of finding happiness in communion with God. Because of all that Christ our Savior has done while we were poor, helpless, needy sinners, God enters into a relationship with

_____

2. Thomas Goodwin, *The Works of Thomas Goodwin* (Grand Rapids: Reformation Heritage Books, 2006), 7:199.

us whereby we may experience exquisite and unending pleasure in Him. We rejoice in the hope of glory. We rejoice in tribulation, but as Goodwin says, "it is a purer and higher joy to rejoice in God Himself."[3]

Defining Communion with God

Outside sacred Scripture, perhaps no better description of communion with God has been given than what John Owen offers in his book by this same title. "Communion with God," Owen says, "is the mutual sharing of those good things which delight each person in that fellowship...and we commune with God in the giving of Himself to us and in our returning to Him all that He requires and accepts by virtue of our union with Christ."[4] So communion with God consists in giving, receiving, and returning; we might even say, a gracious giving, a humble receiving, and a bold returning.

God gives Himself to us through the work of His Son and the work of His Spirit. The Holy Spirit takes the person and work of Christ and causes His beauty, glory, and excellence to become our greatest treasure. The Bible informs our minds with the knowledge of the glory of God, and the Holy Spirit illumines our minds to the spiritual value of that knowledge. He also anoints our affections so that we move beyond mere knowledge about God to the experience of God's glory. Through the Spirit and Word, we are able to savor the sweetness of drawing near to God in the experience of felt love and felt communion. However, communion with God is nothing at all if it's not Trinitarian.

Experiential Christianity is distinctly Trinitarian by

---

3. Ibid., 6:135.
4. John Owen, *The Works of John Owen* (Edinburgh: Banner of Truth Trust, 2000), 2:8.

nature. We can't talk about Christian experience without showing that such experience is anchored once and for all in the Trinity—it is given *by the Father, in His Son,* and realized *through His Spirit.* So, in order to experience the fullness of God, we must explore how we may commune with each member of the Trinity.

We Commune with God the Father in Love

It's easy to see the basis for the subjective experience of God's love in Romans 5:5. The Holy Spirit is its source! And it's just as easy to see the objective basis for faith in the promise of God's love in verses 6 through 10. The Son of God and His death in the place of sinners is its source! But we may easily overlook that both the Spirit's work and Christ's work have their origin in the love of the Father. God the Father is the source of love for His people. Ephesians 2:4–5 says, "But God, who is rich in mercy, for his great love wherewith he loved us, even when we were dead in sins, hath quickened us together with Christ."

Christ and His great work of redemption is a gracious gift rooted in the love of the Father. First Peter 1:3 says, "Blessed be the God and Father of our Lord Jesus Christ, which according to his abundant mercy hath begotten us again unto a lively hope by the resurrection of Jesus Christ from the dead."

The source of the Spirit's regenerating work is also the loving compassion of God the Father. So, when we receive the eternal love of the Father by which He draws us to Himself through His covenant love and faithfulness, we return His love with our sincere devotion and faithfulness (Jer. 31:3).

God does not merely subdue our stubborn wills; His everlasting love wins our wayward affections. "God rests in His love," Zephaniah 3:17 explains. He has no more complaints against us; He has extinguished every one of them in the Son of His love. "Divine wrath is silent, because love has hushed it. Divine justice is silent, because love has satisfied it. Sin is silent, because love has condemned it. Satan is silent, because love has vanquished him. God's love has silenced every voice but its own."[5]

> Oh what power the love of God,
> To silence wrath on sinful clods;
> Love pierced the heart of His own Son,
> To hush the voice of ev'ry one!
>
> Oh what power the love of God,
> To satisfy and silence law;
> Love bruised His Son in my own place,
> To justice fill and give me grace!
>
> Oh what power the love of God,
> To banish sin and fill with awe;
> Love stooped to serve and judge my case,
> To draw me near to see His face!
>
> Oh what power the love of God,
> To vanquish Satan with His Rod;
> Love conquered him—my enemy,
> To put to death all enmity!
>
> Oh what power the love of God,
> To rest and never be at odds;
> Love stills all voices but its own,
> To reign forever from its throne![6]

---

5. Octavius Winslow, *Morning Thoughts* (Grand Rapids: Reformation Heritage Books, 2003), 46.

6. "Love Stills All Voices But Its Own," written by Murray Brett before dawn on Saturday, February 17, 2007, having been awakened

When we receive love from God by faith, we will also return love to Him, and because He rests we may also find rest in Him. We commune with the Father in love, and yet we commune with the Son in grace.

We Commune with God the Son in Grace

According to Romans 5:9–10, we are justified and reconciled through the obedient life and atoning death of Jesus Christ. In every sense, Christ became the guarantee of the Father's love for us. We commune with the Father in love, but He does not communicate one sunbeam of His love to us apart from Christ, and neither do we return or reflect one moonbeam of His love back to Him apart from Christ. Christ is, as Owen says, "the purchased treasury" from which God dispenses all the riches of His great love.[7] I could give no sweeter summary of the proof of all Christ does for us than John Calvin in *The Institutes*, Book 2. Calvin writes,

> ...our whole salvation and all its parts are compre-
> hended in Christ. We should therefore take care not
> to derive the least portion of it from anywhere else. If
> we seek salvation, we are taught by the very name of
> Jesus that it is "of Him." If we seek any other gifts of
> the Spirit, they will be found in *Christ's* anointing. If we
> seek strength, it lies in His dominion; if purity, in His
> conception; if gentleness, it appears in His birth. For
> by His birth He was made like us in all respects that He
> might learn to feel our pain. If we seek redemption, it
> lies in His passion; if acquittal, in His condemnation;

---

by God to pray through Octavius Winslow's devotional thoughts on Zephaniah 3:17 for each person in Grace Baptist Church of Commerce, Georgia. Meter 8.8.8.8.

7. Owen, *The Works of John Owen*, 2:16.

if remission of the curse, in His cross; if satisfaction, in His sacrifice; if purification, in His blood; if reconciliation, in His punishment in our place; if mortification of the flesh, in His tomb; if newness of life, in His resurrection; if immortality, in the same; if inheritance of the Heavenly Kingdom, in His entrance into Heaven; if protection, if security, if abundant supply of all blessings, in His Kingdom; if untroubled expectation of judgment, in the power given to Him to judge. In short, since the rich store of every kind of good abounds in Him, let us drink our fill from this fountain, and from no other.[8]

As Paul says, Christ really is our all-in-all (Col. 3:11). By His substitutionary death, Christ purchased our forgiveness for us; therefore, when we receive His pardon by faith, we return to Him a life free from the condemnation of God, of the law, of sin, of Satan, and of the world. By His perfect obedience to the moral law of God, Christ won for us a standing in grace so that we have free access to God; therefore, when we receive Christ's perfect righteousness, we return the enjoyment of a fellowship with God that entails praise, thanks, adoration, sacrifice, self-denial, and obedience.

In His finished work, Christ offers Himself to us as our final Prophet, Priest, and King. So when we receive Him as our Prophet to teach us, we return devotion to His authoritative and sufficient Word. When we receive Him as our Great High Priest to offer Himself to the Father as a sacrifice and to intercede for us, we return our very lives and our prayers as living sacrifices. And when we receive Him as our King to

---

8. John Calvin, *Calvin's Institutes,* translated by Ford Lewis Battles, edited by John T. McNeill (Louisville: Westminster John Knox Press, 2006), 2.16.19.

rule over us and protect us from all enemies, we return submission and bold service and we live securely in Him.

Thus, we commune with God in love. We commune with Christ in grace. And we commune with the Holy Spirit in comfort.

We Commune with God the Holy Spirit in Comfort
Imagine being told that if you would climb to the top of a certain mountain, you would experience wonder and beauty and vastness as you've never experienced before. The few who've reached the summit say it's a difficult climb, but you decide to go anyway because of the allurement of such incredible beauty. So, one day up you go, and in just a short distance, it proves to be much harder than you'd ever envisioned. Spurred on by the expectation pounding away in your chest, you press on through the cold, thin air. For the last few miles, the ascent is so steep you wind up crawling. With knees and knuckles bleeding, you go on until finally you reach the summit. There, on top of that mountain, you behold beauty and grandeur you never thought possible! You stand with eyes wide open and mouth gaping just trying to soak it all in. You get lost in the wonder of the whole thing. Now, when you return home, what will you do to keep your experience fresh? And what will you do to pass it on to others?

Within the heart of every human soul, God has placed a longing for the experience of something greater than ourselves, a longing for the eternal, a longing for the experience of the glory of God. But how do we attain the experience of the beauty and glory that exists in this eternal God? Is studying Scripture adequate? And if it is, what authority would convince us of its adequacy?[9]

---

9. D. Martyn Lloyd-Jones, adapted from *Authority* (Edinburgh:

Those who trace their spiritual heritage back to the Protestant Reformation and back further to the Apostles look to three sources of authority: *the authority of Christ, the authority of Sacred Scripture,* and *the authority of the Holy Spirit.* But you can know the authority of Christ and the authority of Scripture in a purely intellectual manner. Professing Christians do it all the time! They claim to know Christ and may even be good at defending their knowledge, but they lack the experience of Christ and the experience of the truth because they lack the Spirit's authority and power in their lives.

Romans 5:5 says that God pours His love into our hearts by His Spirit. Experiencing the Spirit's work in shedding God's love abroad in our adversity assures us of God's love for us. John Owen comments,

When we have this experience of the love of God shed abroad in our hearts, *the Spirit* makes every gospel truth as wine well refined to our souls, and the good things of *Christ and the gospel* to be a feast of the best portions possible....[10]According to the sentiments of...profane scoffers, there is no such thing as the shedding abroad of the love of God in our hearts by the Holy Spirit...that the divine promises of a "feast of fat things, and wine well refined," in gospel mercies, are empty and insignificant words—that all the ravishing joys and exultations of spirit...are but fancies and imaginations. But there is no more sacred truth than this, that where Christ is present with believers—where they live with a view of His glory by faith as it is proposed to them—He will give to them, at His own seasons, such intimations of His love, such supplies of His Spirit, such holy joys and

---

The Banner of Truth Trust, 1984), 9.
10. Owen, *The Works of John Owen,* 2:248.

rejoicings, such repose of soul in assurance, as shall refresh their souls, fill them with joy, satisfy them with spiritual delight and quicken them unto all acts of holy communion with Himself.[11]

Experiencing the love of God being poured out by His Spirit is very real. But we scarcely yearn for it and at times may even explain it away because we are not tasting it for ourselves. John Calvin exercised "a judgment of charity" regarding the salvation of church members who maintained a commendable lifestyle, but he also frequently asserted that only a minority receive the preached Word with saving faith. Calvin writes, "For though all, without exception, to whom God's Word is preached, are taught, yet scarce one-in-ten so much as tastes it, yea scarce one-in-a-hundred profits to the extent of being enabled, thereby, to proceed in a right course to the end."[12]

When we receive by faith the manifold works of the Spirit as a Convictor, a Regenerator, an Indweller, an Illuminator, an Anointer, a Sanctifier, a Comforter, and a Sealer we will proceed in a right course to the end and also make returns:

- When we *receive His convicting work*, we confess our sins.

- When we *receive His regenerating work*, we live for the truth and for holiness by the principle of new life He implants in us.

- When we *receive His indwelling work*, we live by His power and not our own, so that in all things God gets the glory.

---

11. Ibid., 1:398–399.
12. Joel Beeke, *The Quest for Full Assurance: The Legacy of Calvin and His Successors* (Carlisle, PA: The Banner of Truth Trust, 1999), 59.

- When we *receive His illuminating work*, we devote ourselves to the wisdom of His Word.

- When we *receive His anointing work*, we pour forth true and holy affections for God.

- When we *receive His sanctifying work*, we repent, mortify our sin and sinfulness, and live a life of devotion to God, striving for holiness in the fear of the Lord.

- When we *receive His comforting work*, we abide in the comfort of His felt presence during our deepest trials to lead us to Christ who is our great sympathetic high priest.

- When we *receive His sealing work*, we bask in the assurance of our full pardon of sin and we direct our attention towards heaven because He dwells within us as the down-payment and the earnest of our future inheritance in glory.

Jesus said that the Father seeks true worshipers and that those who truly worship Him worship in Spirit and in truth (John 4). According to Isaiah 59:21, the Holy Spirit and the written Word of God are inseparably knit together for God's people in His eternal covenant.[13] And, as Owen says, "we might as well go and burn our Bibles as to separate the Spirit from the Word."[14]

God alone determines how He is to be worshiped, and He has plainly declared it to us in His Word. We are not free to worship God as we see fit, nor are we free to use any means we see fit. Man-made religion may have the appearance of wisdom, but it has no value against the indulgence of the flesh (Col. 2:23). So if we are to draw near to God—if

---

13. Owen, *The Works of John Owen*, 3:193.
14. Ibid., 3:192.

we are to experience true happiness in communion with God—we must worship Him by the means that *He* has ordained. David says in Psalm 16:11, "Thou wilt shew me the path of life: in thy presence is fulness of joy; at thy right hand there are pleasures for evermore."

May we make use of every means of grace in the law and the gospel to find our chief happiness in communion with God! And may that communion engage our best thoughts, set on fire our most noble affections, and move our wills to glad-hearted obedience for the glory of God.

May God give Himself to you so that you may make returns on the graces He secured for you. Go and make happy returns by abiding in unassailable peace with God, having once been at enmity with Him. Enjoy the unlimited access you now have with God, having once been shut out of His presence. Exult in your unwavering hope of glory. Rejoice in the unconditional love of God poured out in your sufferings as His method of authenticating your faith. And even more importantly, celebrate God Himself with unrestrained joy!

May God grant that we use every grace He ordains in order to draw near to Him in sweet communion, and may we grow further in glorifying and enjoying Him forever!

DISCUSS THE ISSUES

1. What is the chief end of man? What is the chief fruit and privilege of justifying grace in Romans 5:1–11?

2. Define communion with God. In what specific way do we commune with each member of the Trinity and what specific *returns* do we make as a result of our communion with each?

3. Is it possible that we know Christ and His Word and even be good at defending our knowledge, and yet lack the experience of Christ and the experience of truth? Does God give us the authority to determine how He is to be worshiped or the means that we use in order to worship? What will you think, feel, or do differently in order to obtain such rich and vast treasure as is offered to us in Christ?

SOLVE THE SCENARIO

Gordon grew up in church but had never been discipled. When he moved away to college in Atlanta, he met a young lady and they became quite good friends. She invited him to attend a Bible study where a teacher named Dan taught a large group of young people each Tuesday evening. It was the first time Gordon had ever heard the Bible taught expositionally, and Dan was the first Bible teacher Gordon had ever met who loved God and His Word deeply. He loved personal holiness and exuded a strong passion for the kids to grow in their love for God and in their love for His Word as well. Gordon had been taught that the gospel consisted of the forgiveness of sins and the inheritance of eternal life, but after sitting under Dan's teaching week after week, Gordon knew now that there must be more to a relationship with God than what he had been taught growing up.

Knowing what Gordon was taught in his church growing up, do you think Gordon understands the primary motivation for enjoying communion with God? If you were counseling and discipling Gordon, what would you say to help him grow in fellowship with God?

SIT AT THE FEET OF CHRIST-CENTERED, EXPERIENTIAL TEACHERS

The God You Can Know, by Dan DeHaan (*Level:* Basic)

The Attributes of God, by A. W. Pink (*Level:* Basic to Intermediate)

The Sympathy of Christ, by Octavius Winslow (*Level:* Basic to Intermediate)

Our God, by Octavius Winslow (*Level:* Basic to Intermediate)

God: Coming Face to Face With His Majesty, by John MacArthur Jr. (*Level:* Basic)

Communion with God, by John Owen, edited by R. J. K. Law (*Level:* Basic to Intermediate)

Communion with the Triune God, by John Owen, edited by Kelly M. Kapic and Justin Taylor (*Level:* Intermediate)

Communion with God, by John Owen (*Level:* Intermediate to Difficult)

"The Excellency of Christ," a sermon by Jonathan Edwards (*Level:* Intermediate)

Meditations and Discourses: Concerning The Glory of Christ in His Person, Office and Grace, in volume one of *The Works of John Owen,* by John Owen, (*Level:* Intermediate to Difficult) www.the-highway.com/Glory_contents.html

"Man's Chief End," chapter 1 in *Body of Divinity,* by Thomas Watson (*Level:* Intermediate) www.bpc.org/resources/watson/wsc_wa_001.html

"Of Man's Chief End and Happiness," by Thomas Boston (*Level:* Intermediate) (http://www.the-highway.com/Boston_chiefend.html

The Holy Spirit, by Sinclair B. Ferguson (*Level:* Basic to Intermediate)

Keep in Step with the Spirit, by J. I. Packer (*Level:* Basic to Intermediate)

Psalm 131

Lord, my heart is not haughty, nor mine eyes lofty: neither do I exercise myself in great matters, or in things too high for me. ²Surely I have behaved and quieted myself, as a child that is weaned of his mother: my soul is even as a weaned child. ³Let Israel hope in the LORD from henceforth and for ever.

CHAPTER TWO

The Grace of Humility

I WAS RAISED IN rural Georgia. When I turned thirteen, a good friend of my dad's named David Maddox gave my brother John and me a puppy. He turned out to be the pick of the litter. Part bulldog, part Florida Cur, he grew up to be a big dog, about eighty pounds. His tail was stubbed, his body cream colored, and the tips of his ears and nose, black. He looked almost exactly like a polar bear, and you guessed it—we named him Bear.

Bear was a great dog for two teenage boys growing up in the country. We used him to work cattle and hogs on our farm, and he would trail almost any animal in the woods: deer, squirrels, rabbits, you name it. But that's just the half of it. Bear was great fun just to play with. As kids, John and I spent hours upon hours tussling around with him in the yard. He was really sneaky, too. When we weren't looking, Bear would sneak up behind one of us and fleabite us right on the rear end. He never hurt us, but when we turned to scold him in our flea-bitten moment of surprise, it was as if he was grinning afterwards because he had pulled one over on us.

We think of some sins as really terrible evil: envy, anger, greed, hatred, drunkenness,... and these are all very horrible sins. But compared to pride, *these are mere fleabites.* No other sin affects us at the very core of our being like pride, and no other sin results in a completely anti-God state like pride.

Perhaps no one has depicted the depth of pride outside sacred Scripture better than John Milton. In *Paradise Lost*, Milton illustrates raw undiluted pride as Satan says, "In Hell we are at least free...and...my choice to reign is worth ambition, though in Hell—Better to reign in Hell, than to serve in Heav'n."[1]

In our study on using the means of grace, we want to address the humility of faith at the beginning, because without faith it is impossible to please God (Heb. 11:6). In order to profit spiritually from our personal study or from the public ministry of the Word of God, we must receive what we hear with simple faith (Heb. 4:2). So, from Psalm 131, we are going to look at pride and its counterpoint, humble faith. Charles Spurgeon once said of Psalm 131 that although this is one of the shortest Psalms to read, it is one of the longest to learn.

A PICTURE OF PRIDE

In verse 1, David gives a three-part picture of pride: *a heart that is lifted up, eyes that are haughty,* and *a concern for matters that ought not to concern us.*

A Heart that is Lifted Up

There's a multitude of sins we may commit, but to lift up our heart against God or to live without expressing our dependence upon Him as God is the greatest sin we could possibly commit. It is a sin for which no punishment is too great.

---

1. John Milton, *Paradise Lost*, edited by Barbara Lewalski (Malden, MA: Blackwell Publishing, 2007), 20.

Hence Christ's death upon the cross for such awful evil! In Isaiah 42:8, God says, "I *am* the LORD: that is my name: and my glory will I not give to another." John Calvin said, "God cannot bear with seeing His glory appropriated by the creature in even the smallest degree. Therefore the sacrilegious arrogance of those who praise themselves and obscure His glory is absolutely intolerable to God."[2]

Henry Martyn was an incredibly gifted teacher. He gave up a career in the language department at Cambridge University to become a missionary to Persia in the early 1800's. Shortly after his arrival in Persia, he was shown a picture of Jesus bowing down to Mohammed and he broke into uncontrollable weeping. His friends had never seen him behave that way and thought the heat might have gotten to him. However, he explained that he could not even bear to live if his Savior was so dishonored. A single sentence written by Henry Martyn to a friend shows a kind and degree of self-awareness that few people possess. He wrote, "Men frequently admire me, and I am pleased; but I abhor the pleasure that I feel."[3]

No doubt, we often confess the sin of pride, but are we really convinced of its true nature? Charles Bridges once said that "pride lifts up the heart against God, and it contends for supremacy with Him."[4] After reading Bridges' comments, C. J. Mahaney, another very self-aware pastor, said that he no longer feels it adequate to simply confess pride. He

---

2. John Calvin, *Commentary on the Psalms* (Albany, OR: Books for the Ages, 1998), 1:33; reworded for clarity.

3. Charles Bridges, *The Christian Ministry* (Carlisle, PA: The Banner of Truth Trust, 1991), 153.

4. Charles Bridges, *Proverbs* (Wheaton, IL: Crossway Books, 2001), 129.

said that it changed his entire perspective so that he now confesses that he is contending for supremacy with Christ. And C. J. added that "it is not if pride exists in our lives; it is rather, where."

Is that your perspective? Are you convinced of the sin of pride? Are you aware of ways you manage your life for your own glory and rob God of His? Do you see how you contend with God for supremacy? There is no sin to which we are more prone or of which we are more blind than pride. It is the root and motivation of all other sin. It was the cause of the very first sin here on earth. When Satan tempted Adam and Eve, he first cast doubt in their minds regarding God's faithfulness to rule over them for their greatest good. Then he lured them away from God by promising that they would become like God and be able to rule their own lives for their own greatest good. Consequently, we've been contending with God ever since. What deception! What blindness!

Lifting up our hearts against God is our greatest struggle. Without exception, it's at the heart of every sin we commit: selfishness, discontentment, covetousness, lust, and envy. Why? Because we are dissatisfied with where God has us in life. Contending with God for supremacy is also at the heart of fear, worry, anxiety, doubt, and manipulation. And when we commit these kinds of sins, it's evident that we're not confident that God is able or willing to work all things together for our greatest good. Therefore, we lift up our heart against God. Jonathan Edwards once wrote,

> Pride takes many forms and shapes and encompasses the heart like the layers of an onion—when you pull off one layer, there is another underneath. Therefore, we need to have the greatest watch imaginable over our hearts with respect to pride and to cry out earnestly to

the Great Searcher of our hearts for His help. He who trusts his own heart is a fool.[5]

Do you know your heart? Do you recognize the ways in which you lift your heart against God? Proverbs 16:5 says, "Every one that is proud in heart is an abomination to the LORD." No stronger language can be found in sacred Scripture than what is employed against the sin of pride! Why? Because the proud person contends with God for supremacy and there's no fouler way to offend God.

Eyes that are too Haughty

The second part of David's picture of pride is *inordinate ambition*. What is rejected is the sin of being supercilious. To be supercilious is to have an air of contempt about us, an air of superiority. The word comes from the Latin word for eyebrow. Agur gives a good description of the sin of pride from this perspective in Proverbs 30:11–13. He says that there are some sinners who curse or speak with contempt against their father and mother. They are pure in their own eyes, but not at all pure in the eyes of God. Agur adds that their "eyelids are lifted up." They are simply the best and they look down on everyone else because they are superior in their estimation of themselves.

In 1 Corinthians 4:7, Paul asks this question of the proud: "What hast thou that thou didst not receive? now if thou didst receive it, why dost thou glory, as if thou hadst not received it?" The word that Paul uses for pride in verse 6 means to be puffed up, distended, over-inflated. This is to be

---

5. Jonathan Edwards, *The Works of Jonathan Edwards* (Edinburgh: The Banner of Truth Trust, 1995), 1:399; reworded for clarity.

so filled up with self that you are ready to burst. The eyes of the proud are too haughty; they are too lofty.

Now we must guard against misunderstanding here. There is nothing wrong with striving to be the best we possibly can be at what we do in order to be the most useful that we can in the kingdom of God. It is not pride in the wrong sense when we do a good job and are aware that we have done a good job. We all should desire to hear Christ say, "Well done, good and faithful servant; thou hast been faithful over a few things...enter into the joy of thy lord" (Matt. 25:23). Problems arise, however, when we are driven by so much ambition that we compete with everyone else.

Pride is essentially competitive. It does not take pleasure in simply doing something, or being someone, or having something. Pride takes pleasure in doing better, being better, and having more than everyone else. C. S. Lewis has a chapter on pride called "The Great Sin" in his book *Mere Christianity*. He writes,

> It is comparison that makes us proud: the pleasure of being above the rest. Once the element of competition is gone, pride is gone. Pride will lead you to take a spot in the band, in the play, or on the team not because you want the position, but just because you want to prove that you are better than the other person. Greed may drive a person into competition if there's not enough to go around; but the proud person, even when he has got more than he can possibly want, will try to get still more, just to assert his power.[6]

6. C. S. Lewis, *Mere Christianity*, (New York, NY: HarperCollins, 2001), 122.

How easily we cross the line between trying to be the best we possibly can to trying to be better than everyone else!

A Concern for Matters that Ought Not to Concern Us

The third part of the picture of pride is *presumption*: an arrogant assumption of privileged status, privileged access, or privileged information. Surely we ought to seek to know all that we can know about God and about life, especially the Christian life. But we can have too great a concern for things that ought not to concern us. This manifests itself as a concern for things that are really not ours to know or understand. Deuteronomy 29:29 says that "the secret things belong unto the LORD our God: but those things which are revealed belong unto us and to our children for ever, that we may do all the words of this law." It's been said that many wishing to know too much have failed to know anything good at all, or wishing to be too great have failed to be anything good at all.[7]

The landscape of Scripture is scattered with men who sinned presumptuously. Uzziah was a king, but that was not enough for him. He desired to usurp the office of priest and offer incense in the Temple. God struck him with leprosy and cast him out. Diotrophes was a teacher, but that was not enough for him: he wanted a place of prominence in the church. He was divisive and cast others out. Satan was an angel, but it was not enough. He wanted to be in the place of God Himself, and God cast him down. Hezekiah was also a king, mighty in prayer and used mightily of God. He extended the boundaries of Israel and many nations paid tribute to Israel as a result, but he did not make returns to the

---

7. Charles Spurgeon, *The Treasury of David* (Grand Rapids, MI: Baker Book House, 1984), 7:87; quote adapted.

Lord according to the benefits which the Lord had shown him. He did not respond to God's mercy and kindness. His heart was also lifted up with pride. He became sick and very near death; however, Hezekiah repented. He humbled himself and prayed, and God raised him up.

Consider also Beatrice Webb. She and her husband were two of the most influential members of the Fabian Society in England. The Fabian Society sought to spread socialism through non-revolutionary means. In the 1930s, Beatrice and her husband went to Russia and afterwards assured the world that Joseph Stalin was building a paradise. Actually, Stalin was slaughtering millions of poor Russian people to build his own so-called paradise. When Beatrice Webb and her husband returned, they were interviewed by the press and a number of world leaders. Beatrice admitted that she was nervous, but whenever she was nervous, she would say to herself, "You're the cleverest member of one of the cleverest families in the cleverest class of the cleverest nation in the world, so what have you got to be afraid of?" What vain conceit![8]

There's also G. Gordon Liddy. He was one of the Watergate conspirators, along with his colleague Chuck Colson. Like the prodigal son, Colson came to himself during the whole ordeal, recognizing his need for Christ and repenting. Compare that with what G. Gordon Liddy once said, some believe in response to Colson's conversion: "I have found within myself all I need and all I shall ever need. I am a man of great faith, but my faith is in George Gordon Liddy. I have never failed me."[9]

---

8. Geoff Thomas, sermon on "Philippians 2:3–4," www.alfred placechurch.org.uk/sermons/phil13.htm.
   9. Ibid.

Do you see yourself in any of these examples? We hate to admit it, but too often we can.

THE PROOF OF HUMILITY

In Psalm 131:1, David says that he had overcome his pride, and in verse two, he gives proof of it: "Surely I have behaved and quieted myself, as a child that is weaned of his mother: my soul is even as a weaned child."

David describes how he has become free of his pride. By God's grace, he weaned his soul from self-seeking, and now he describes his soul like a weaned child.

Do you know God? Have you met Him? In God, we come up against something which in every respect is greater than we are.[10] God is immeasurably superior to us and unless you understand that—unless it affects you to the point that you cry out to Him for His grace in the gospel of Jesus Christ—you do not yet know Him as you ought.

C. S. Lewis raises an important question when he asks, "How is it that people who are quite obviously eaten up with pride can say they believe in God and appear to themselves very religious?" Lewis responds, "I am afraid it means that they are worshiping an imaginary God." "The real test," he says, "of knowing God and being in the presence of God is that you forget about yourself altogether or see yourself as a small, dirty object."[11]

How may we wean ourselves from self? How may we forget ourselves? In 1 Corinthians 4:3–4, Paul says, "But with me it is a very small thing that I should be judged of you, or of man's judgment: yea, I judge not mine own self.

---

10. Lewis, *Mere Christianity*, 124.
11. Ibid., 125.

For I know nothing by myself; yet am I not hereby justified: but he that judgeth me is the Lord."

The word for *judge* here means to investigate and render a verdict. Paul's identity was in no way tied to what others thought of him or to what he thought of himself. Paul refused to fall into our modern day self-esteem trap. Rather, he esteemed the grace of God in the finished work of Christ and cried out in Galatians 2:20–21, "I am crucified with Christ: nevertheless I live; yet not I, but Christ liveth in me: and the life which I now live in the flesh I live by the faith of the Son of God, who loved me, and gave himself for me. I do not frustrate the grace of God: for if righteousness come by the law, then Christ is dead in vain."

When we go to someone for counsel because we feel we've been unduly criticized by another person, the most common first piece of advice is this: "It shouldn't matter what others think. The only thing that matters is what you think." That is the way we are taught to deal with criticism and the low self-esteem that results. "Esteem yourself! Think more highly of yourself; after all you really are a great person!" But that's not what Paul did. His confidence didn't come from himself, but from Christ. His acceptance didn't come from himself, but from Christ. Paul was not puffed up with himself; he was filled up with Christ. The only court that mattered to Paul was God's, and that's where he lived. Paul did not say, "I did a bad job, so I must be a bad person," or "I did a good job, so I must be a good person." He understood that God accepts His children on the basis of Christ's work in the gospel. God has taken our sin and credited it to Christ and has taken Christ's righteousness and credited it to us. Paul lived out of the gospel. That is where he found his identity.[12]

Are you still waiting for a verdict? If so, then you are not yet weaned from self and are still working to fill up the emptiness in your life in order to make you feel better about yourself.

If you live for self-esteem and good feelings about yourself, you will never measure up; you can never be good enough and you will often use the "kudos" and respect you seek from others to fill the void that is left by not being filled with Christ. If that describes you, I plead with you to stop. Stop trying to measure up and start realizing that Christ obtained the full measure of God's acceptance by His obedient life and His substitutionary death. Learn gospel acceptance. Learn what it means to be accepted in God's court by virtue of what Christ has done for you. Learn to live out of the gospel every day.

Our egos will never be satisfied until clothed in gospel humility. And the essence of gospel humility is not thinking less of ourselves, but thinking more of Christ than ourselves. Then we will be weaned from ourselves and we will also think more highly of others. We will not be puffed up, but we will be filled up with Jesus Christ. In Romans 4, Paul uses David as an example of one who has learned gospel humility and gospel acceptance and, as a result, he persevered in hope.

PERSEVERANCE IN HOPE

In Psalm 131:3 David writes, "Let Israel hope in the Lord from henceforth and for ever."

---

12. Timothy Keller, sermon tape entitled, "Blessed Self-Forgetfulness."

Do you know what it is to find real relief from your pride because you've put your hope in God? Being emptied of self and filled with Christ causes us to persevere in hope.

We all know how ugly pride is in others, but it's just as ugly in us. Our problem is that we don't see or recognize it nearly so well in ourselves as we do in others, and even when we do, we treat our own pride like a mere fleabite instead of the horribly infected and infecting wound it really is. Pride is the first, the worst, and the most prevalent of all sins; yet we have the tendency to treat it as if it is nothing at all, at least when it is in us.

The first step in getting rid of the sin of pride is realizing that you are proud. And if you don't believe you're proud, you're much more proud than you know.

The great old devotional commentator, Matthew Henry, wrote a little book called, *The Quest for Meekness and Quietness of Spirit;* it's well worth reading again and again. In it he says,

> Humility softens the soul like wax that we may receive the impression of the seal, whether it be "for doctrine, for reproof or correction, or for training in righteousness." Humility opens our spiritual ears to discipline, silences the objections of the flesh, and suppresses the risings of the carnal mind against the Word of God. It agrees that the law of God is good and esteems all its precepts to be right even when they give the greatest check to our fleshly pride.[13]

When the grace of humility is at work in us, we silently submit our souls to Scripture like a weaned child. We cease

---

13. Matthew Henry, *The Quest for Meekness and Quietness of Spirit* (Morgan, PA: Soli Deo Gloria, 1996), 19.

serving the interests of self in order to serve the interests of God and of others. So, by the Spirit's grace, clothe yourself in the grace of humility and gospel acceptance. And as you grow up in receiving acceptance from God in the gospel, you will surely accept and serve others in the power of that same gospel. Come to Christ so that He might give you the grace of humility and gospel acceptance—and keep on coming in order to live in communion with Him.

DISCUSS THE ISSUES

1. Define pride. Discuss various ways in which we might "contend with God for supremacy."

2. Earlier Christians were careful to categorize sin into "root sins, trunk sins, branch sins, and so on." How is pride to blame for so many other sins (discontent, covetousness, lust, worry, etc.)? Explain how pride is essentially competitive. How can we fail to know or do anything good at all by sinning presumptuously? Why is it that we so easily see pride in others and do not see it in ourselves?

3. What is the proof of humility? What is gospel humility and why will our ego never be satisfied until it's clothed with gospel humility? Read Hebrews 4:2 and explain how faith works to cause us to profit from private study as well as the public preaching of sacred Scripture.

4. In light of your character and calling in life, what are your main temptations to pride?

SOLVE THE SCENARIO

Kurt and Kay have been married for twenty years. Even after so many years, their relationship continues to suffer from several major struggles. When Kay doesn't meet Kurt's expectations, or when Kurt crosses Kay, they each experience a high degree of frustration with one another and occasionally even anger. When they discuss the cause of their frustration or anger, both seek to justify their actions and shift blame, so their discussion often provokes a greater degree of frustration and anger than the offense itself. Kurt claims to be open-minded, but Kay says he seems to be open to listening to everyone but her. She says Kurt often seeks to get off the hook by saying that it's her manner or her tone of voice or her timing that provokes him. Kurt believes his expectations of Kay are not sinful at all, and he's often gone to passages in the Bible to show Kay clear principles that his expectations of her honor God. He seems to think that Kay may not be willing to serve him as she ought, or when she does seek to serve him, she often serves in the strength of her will. Kurt believes if she had a change of heart towards him, she wouldn't have any trouble at all even exceeding his expectations of her.

Kurt and Kay are at loggerheads with one another and are seeking help from you. Let's say you and your spouse have been married for forty years now and have worked through similar issues about twenty years ago. Kurt and Kay have asked the two of you for help to get on track relationally. After telling you their story, they ask you to help them identify what each of their own besetting sins are. They also ask what each must do to serve one another as Christ would have them and how to discuss their offenses or conflict when they arise without causing greater provocation. What would you say to them, starting with identifying their real besetting sins and weaknesses?

SIT AT THE FEET OF CHRIST-CENTERED, EXPERIENTIAL TEACHERS

Humility: True Greatness, by C. J. Mahaney (*Level:* Basic)

Humility: The Forgotten Virtue, by Wayne Mack (*Level:* Basic)

"Blessed Are the Poor in Spirit," November 12 reading in *Morning Thoughts,* by Octavius Winslow (*Level:* Basic to Intermediate) *http://gracegems.org/WINSLOW/November.htm*

"Showing how difficult the practice of humility is made, by the general spirit and temper of the world. How Christianity requires us to live contrary to the world," Chapter 17 in *A Serious Call to a Devout and Holy Life,* by William Law (*Level:* Intermediate) *http://gracegems.org/book4/William_Law.htm*

The Quest for Meekness and Quietness of Spirit, by Matthew Henry (*Level:* Intermediate)

"This Monster Pride, This Hellish Thing," in *Anne Dutton's Letters on Spiritual Subjects,* by Anne Dutton (*Level:* Basic to Intermediate) www.gracegems.org/Dutton/pride.htm

"What Is Humility?" *Taste and See* article by John Piper (*Level:* Basic) www.desiringgod.org/ResourceLibrary/TasteAndSee/ByDate/1999/1140_What_Is_Humility/

"Assurance and Humility," by A. A. Hodge (*Level:* Basic to Intermediate) www.puritansermons.com/reformed/ahodge1.htm

"Humility," by William Romaine (*Level:* Intermediate) www.eternallifeministries.org/wr_humility.htm

"Undiscerned Spiritual Pride," by Jonathan Edwards in *Some Thoughts Concerning the Present Revival of Religion* (*Level:* Intermediate)

Psalm 32:1–11

Blessed is he whose transgression is forgiven, whose sin is covered. ²Blessed is the man unto whom the LORD imputeth not iniquity, and in whose spirit there is no guile. ³When I kept silence, my bones waxed old through my roaring all the day long. ⁴For day and night thy hand was heavy upon me: my moisture is turned into the drought of summer. Selah. ⁵I acknowledged my sin unto thee, and mine iniquity have I not hid. I said, I will confess my transgressions unto the LORD; and thou forgavest the iniquity of my sin. Selah. ⁶For this shall every one that is godly pray unto thee in a time when thou mayest be found: surely in the floods of great waters they shall not come nigh unto him. ⁷Thou art my hiding place; thou shalt preserve me from trouble; thou shalt compass me about with songs of deliverance. Selah. ⁸I will instruct thee and teach thee in the way thou shalt go: I will guide thee with mine eye. ⁹Be ye not as the horse, or as the mule, which have no understanding: whose mouth must be held in with bit and bridle, lest they come near unto thee. ¹⁰Many sorrows shall be to the wicked: but he that trusteth in the LORD, mercy shall compass him about. ¹¹Be glad in the LORD, and rejoice, ye righteous: and shout for joy, all ye that are upright in heart.

CHAPTER THREE

The Grace of Confession

THERE'S A FAMOUS illustration by a French philosopher named Jean Paul Sartre that goes like this. Imagine you're in a room and you see a keyhole with light pouring from it. You bend down to look through the keyhole and you see people doing things, but they don't know that you're watching them. Then, you hear footsteps behind you, and suddenly you realize that you too are being watched and that you feel deeply ashamed. Since the Fall of Adam and Eve, that's the way we live. We live knowing that others are watching. Rather than living freely in the presence of God and for God, we live in the presence of others and for others because nothing is more unbearable than being unable to control what people see and know about us. Within the heart of every human soul is a deep sense of need to cover. For another person to have complete access to what we're thinking, how we are feeling, and how we're living is unbearable.[1]

What would it be like not to have to cover anymore? What would it be like not to worry about what others think

---

1. Jean-Paul Sartre, *Being and Nothingness*, translated by Hazel Barnes (New York: Washington Square Press, 1993), 369–370; additional comments summarized from Timothy Keller from a sermon tape on Psalm 32.

of us—not to have to shade their view of us or to spin or to put up a front or to hide? In Psalm 32,[2] David says that the most blessed state in which to live is not to cover anymore, but to have God cover us. When we practice the grace of confession, we will live in the blessedness of having our sins covered by Christ.

THE NECESSITY OF CONFESSING, NOT COVERING, YOUR SIN

There's hardly anyone who doesn't know the background of the thirty-second Psalm. It's David's adultery with Bathsheba and his murder of Uriah. But, I wonder, do you know what happened afterwards? As soon as David filled his mind with Bathsheba's beauty, he laid aside the danger of sin's delight. Allured by his lust, he stopped carefully considering sin's guilt and all its corrupting influences. Then, 2 Samuel 12:9 says, David grew to "despise the commandment of the LORD." For a whole year he denied his sin. Knowing our own struggles with remaining sin, it's not too hard to imagine that David tried to go about life as usual for a whole year. He went to the temple as usual, prayed as usual, and read the bedside copy of his Bible at night as usual. However, he refused to acknowledge his sin; for an entire year, he lived in a state of carnal security, a state of false assurance. During that time, his body wasted away. He says that his bones ached, perhaps as if he had gout, which Charles Spurgeon argued is ten times worse than arthritis. Held hostage by his sin, he was like a prisoner of war, forced to work in extreme

---

2. Psalm 32 is the second of seven penitential psalms—psalms expressing the confession and repentance of sin. In order, they are Psalm 6, 32, 38, 51, 102, 130, and 143.

heat, and the awfulness of his experience pressed in upon him day and night.

Why was he in this awful condition? Why so long out of fellowship with God? Because his sin deceived him into acting as if nothing happened at all. When your sin deceives you, a wise old pastor once said, even "though your heart may have a settled and fixed hatred for sin, your imagination may be so frequently, powerfully, and constantly solicited by sin that your affections become secretly enticed and entangled."[3]

After a year of covering and refusing to confess his sin, God sent the prophet Nathan. David did not confess his sin of his own accord. It took the stern and caring confrontation of a man of God to show David what was going on in his heart so that he finally stopped covering.

In Psalm 32:1, David says that a person whose sin is covered by God is a blessed person, but in verses 1 through 5, he creates a picture for us of the opposite of this state of blessedness. When we cover our sin, as David did for a time, we conceal it from others. For a while, we hide it. The same word is used in verse 5, but at this point, he has stopped hiding. He's no longer silent about his sin and there's no longer deceit found in his spirit. He simply and clearly confesses his sin.

Genesis 2 retells the story of the creation of Adam and Eve. At the end of the chapter, God joins them together in marriage and they become one flesh and verse 25 says, "They were both naked, and were not ashamed." But Adam and Eve sinned by doing what God had specifically prohibited. After they ate of the forbidden fruit, Genesis 3:7–8 tell us, "And the eyes of them both were opened, and they knew

---

3. Owen, *The Works of John Owen*, 6:246.

that they were naked; and they sewed fig leaves together, and made themselves aprons. And they heard the voice of the LORD God walking in the garden in the cool of the day: and Adam and his wife hid themselves from the presence of the LORD."

Before their sin, Adam and Eve never hid. They had no need to; they were clothed with moral and spiritual beauty. However, they sinned and plunged the whole human race into sin with them so that whenever we sin, we also hide because of our guilt and shame. Our covering is due to the loss of our moral and spiritual beauty and our sense of innocence. We cover because we want to control what others see and, like David, easily imagine that we can also hide our sin from God.

How do we hide? In what ways do we sew fig leaves to cover the guilt for what we do and the feeling of shame for what we are? First, like Adam, we shift blame. Blame shifting may well be the consummate indication that we are depending upon our own imagined goodness and seeking to cover for ourselves. "Adam! Who said that you were naked? Have you been eating from the forbidden tree, Adam?" He answers, "But Lord, it was this woman Thou gavest me."

Second, like Eve, we extenuate the circumstances of our sin—we tone it down. And when that takes place, our mind is drawn away from its duties as the watchman of our souls, and so our affections are enticed into sin.[4] "Eve! What is this you have done?" She answers, "I was misinformed; I was misled by that serpent Thou didst allow into the garden."

Working as a journalist in India, Malcolm Muggeridge left his residence one evening to go to a nearby river for a

---

4. Ibid., 6:245.

swim. As he entered the water, across the river he saw an Indian woman from the village who had come to bathe. Muggeridge impulsively felt the allurement of the moment. Temptation stormed his mind. He had lived with this sort of struggle for years but had somehow fought it off in honor of his commitment to his wife, Kitty. On this occasion, however, he wondered if he could cross the line of marital fidelity. He struggled just for a moment and then swam furiously toward the woman, literally trying to outdistance his conscience. His mind fed him the fantasy that stolen waters would be sweet, and he swam the harder for it. Now he was just two or three feet away from her, and as he emerged from the water, the desire that had held him in its grip was completely shattered by the horror he observed. She was a leper! The experience left Muggeridge trembling and he exclaimed under his breath, "Dirty lecherous woman!" But then a greater horror overcame him. It was not the woman who was lecherous and given over to excessive desire; it was he. It was his own heart.[5]

How much like Malcolm Muggeridge and Adam and Eve we are. We're drawn away by our own sinful desires and we shift the blame. Or, like David, we're enticed and drawn away by our lusts and act as if nothing ever happened at all.

There are dozens of other ways we may cover. We ignore, justify, and excuse our sin. We indulge in pleasure. We eat or drink as a way of lessening the nagging consequences of our sin. We shop to make us feel better about ourselves. We coddle ourselves in all sorts of ways. We make ourselves feel better by criticizing others, or we compensate by doing

---

5. Ravi Zacharias, *Can Man Live Without God* (Dallas: Word Publishing, 1994), 136–137.

enough good to outweigh the bad. We say that we don't understand the Bible or a certain Bible teacher, and the problem is often not mental, but moral and spiritual. We try to out-give our guilt. Some compensate by being overly sensitive and easily hurt; some by being angry, bitter, and controlling.[6] John Owen adds that we use the hope of pardon or the promise that we will some day repent to hide our sin and guilt, or we extenuate our sin.[7] We say things like: "It was a bad day; I was under a lot of stress; it just took me by surprise." We make a resolution starting tomorrow simply so we might enjoy the pleasure of our lust today. There are a thousand excuses more and we must know the particular ways we are prone to cover. We must get to know ourselves. We must get to know our own heart, and when we do, we begin to uncover the sinful motives behind our sinful actions so that we confess not only the actions themselves, but also the sinful condition of our heart.

The remedy for covering is confession. In verse 5, David says, "I acknowledged my sin unto thee, and mine iniquity have I not hid. I said, I will confess my transgressions unto the Lord." First John 1:8–9 says, "If we say that we have no sin, we deceive ourselves, and the truth is not in us. If we confess our sins, he is faithful and just to forgive us our sins, and to cleanse us from all unrighteousness." The word *confession* literally means "to say the same thing." When we confess our sin, we say the same thing about our sin that God does; we view it as God does. We agree with Him regarding the horror of it. Owen writes that we do not take one step toward finding relief from God until we begin to

---

6. Adapted from Timothy Keller, sermon tape on Psalm 32.
7. Owen, *The Works of John Owen*, 6:249.

see ourselves the way He sees us. By nature, we lack what God must give: a due sense of our sin. And Owen adds that it's possible to have such a sense of our sin as to have "a fire shut up in our bones," but never "find peace with God or relief from our sin because we refuse to come to a 'free...acknowledgment' of our sin. An acknowledgment which sees our sin as 'rebellion against God's sovereignty, as an opposition to His holiness, and as acting independently from Him who is our Creator.'"[8]

In the mid-1700's, David Brainerd served as a pioneer missionary to the American Indians in Crossweeksung, New Jersey. He left a tremendous legacy for countless other missionaries and pastors. When he was twenty years old, he became alive to a terrifying sense of the holiness of God. In his diary he wrote,

> It pleased God...to give me all of a sudden such a sense of my danger, and the wrath of God, that I stood amazed, and my former good frames which I had pleased myself with, all presently vanished; and, from the view I had of my sin and vileness, I was much distressed all day, fearing the vengeance of God would soon overtake me. I was much dejected, and kept much alone, and sometimes begrudged the birds and beasts their happiness, because they were not exposed to eternal misery, as I evidently saw I was. And thus I lived day to day, being frequently in distress.[9]

Brainerd attended preaching more often and paid closer attention to improving himself morally, but one morning as he was walking, he saw how foolish he had been. He was

---

8. Ibid., 6:398–399.
9. Edwards, *The Works of Jonathan Edwards,* 2:317.

brought to a place of recognizing himself to be totally lost. Then salvation was opened up to him and he saw unspeakable glory in God and the peace of Christ flooded his soul.[10] In a similar way, Brainerd said what King David says in the first five verses of Psalm 32. "I uncovered and God covered."

We must not only confess our sin; we must confess our self-righteousness, our works-righteousness, our fig-leaves, our hiding, our covering. God will relate to us only when we stop covering ourselves and allow Him to cover us with the perfect righteousness of Christ. David says in Psalm 32:1–2, "Blessed is he whose transgression is forgiven, whose sin is covered. Blessed is the man unto whom the LORD imputeth not iniquity."

Paul quotes these verses in Romans 4, but rather than simply stating Psalm 32:2 in the negative, Paul adds: "But to him that worketh not, but believeth on him that justifieth the ungodly, his faith is counted [credited] for righteousness. Even as David also describeth the blessedness of the man, unto whom God imputeth [credits] righteousness without works."

In salvation, a dual exchange takes place. God takes our sin and credits it to Christ's account and He takes Christ's righteousness and credits it to our account. Three Old Testament passages depict very graphically the exchange of Christ's righteousness for our unrighteousness. The first is in Ezekiel 16. In verses 4 through 8 God says to Israel:

> And as for thy nativity, in the day thou wast born thy navel was not cut, neither wast thou washed in water to supple thee; thou wast not salted at all, nor swaddled at all. None eye pitied thee, to do any of these unto thee, to have compassion upon thee; but thou wast cast out

---

10. Ibid.

in the open field, to the loathing of thy person, in the day that thou wast born. And when I passed by thee, and saw thee polluted in thine own blood, I said unto thee when thou wast in thy blood, Live.... Now when I passed by thee, and looked upon thee, behold, thy time was the time of love; and I spread my skirt over thee, and covered thy nakedness: yea, I sware unto thee, and entered into a covenant with thee, saith the Lord GOD, and thou becamest mine.

The second is in Zechariah 3:1–5:

And he showed me Joshua the high priest standing before the angel of the LORD, and Satan standing at his right hand to resist him. And the LORD said unto Satan, The LORD rebuke thee, O Satan; even the LORD that hath chosen Jerusalem rebuke thee: is not this a brand plucked out of the fire? Now Joshua was clothed with filthy garments, and stood before the angel. And he answered and spake unto those that stood before him, saying, Take away the filthy garments from him. And unto him he said, Behold, I have caused thine iniquity to pass from thee, and I will clothe thee with change of raiment. And I said, Let them set a fair mitre upon his head. So they set a fair mitre upon his head, and clothed him with garments. And the angel of the LORD stood by.

Then in Isaiah 61:10, Isaiah says, "I will greatly rejoice in the LORD, my soul shall be joyful in my God; for he hath clothed me with the garments of salvation, he hath covered me with the robe of righteousness."

John Newton captures the wonders of free grace to completely satisfy all God's just demands in pardoning our

sin in his great hymn, "Let Us Love and Sing and Wonder."
He writes,

> Let us wonder; grace and justice
> Join to point to mercy's store;
> When through grace our trust is,
> Justice smiles and asks no more.

Samuel Gandy also writes of complete forgiveness we
possess in Christ in his hymn, "I Hear the Accuser Roar":

> I hear the accuser roar
> Of ills that I have done,
> I know them well and thousands more,
> Jehovah knoweth none.

How does God accomplish this great work so that He no
longer counts any of our sins against us? By imputing our
sin to Christ and imputing Christ's righteousness to us. The
word impute is an accounting term, and in order to better
understand its meaning we need to contrast justification
with the new birth.

So that you don't mistake the importance of this
distinction, consider the following illustrations with me.
Every sport and career has its technical language. Golf has
its pars, birdies, and bogeys; computers have their gigahertz
and gigabytes. Well, let's say that your boss came to you on
Friday afternoon and said that he's given some thought to
your proposal for advancement in the company, and that he
also has a proposal. He has a new project and he thinks that
you're just the right person for it. So he gives you a 300-page
technical manual and a stack of files and says that he wants
you to familiarize yourself with it over the weekend so that
you and he might discuss it the first thing Monday morning.
What would you do? I can tell you what you would do! If

THE GRACE OF CONFESSION   53

you're interested in your growth in the company, you'll take it home and study it carefully. You'll probably even get on the internet or go to the library and do some above and beyond research. Why? Because you want to please your boss and advance in the company!

Sacred Scripture also has its technical language for salvation, and in order to grow in grace we must become better acquainted with its rich vocabulary. Salvation is not one indistinguishable work. It's variegated; it's multi-faceted. Salvation has acts such as calling, regeneration, adoption, and justification, and it has processes such as faith, repentance, and sanctification.

To contrast justification and the new birth, we need to define each term biblically and clearly. The new birth is a change in the governing principle of our souls. In the new birth, God takes away the dominion of sin from our lives. He transfers us out of the realm where sin reigns into the realm where grace, truth, and righteousness reign.[11] The new birth is an actual change in our nature—it involves the enlightenment of our minds in the knowledge of Christ and the renewal of our wills so that we eagerly embrace the work of Christ in the gospel.

On the other hand, justification is a change in legal status or legal standing, not a change in nature.[12] The *Catechism for Boys and Girls* describes justification this way: justification is God regarding sinners as if they have never sinned. A catechism for older children and adults says that "justification is an act of God's free grace, by which He pardons all our sins, and accepts us as righteous in His

---

11. Cf. Rom. 6:1–14; Eph. 4:22–24; Col. 3:8–11.
12. Cf. Rom. 3:21–5:21.

sight, only for the righteousness of Christ imputed to us, and received by faith alone."[13] When we confess our sin at the time of our conversion, God makes a once-for-all-time declaration that He no longer counts our sin against us but that He counts us as righteous in His sight on the basis of all Christ has done for us. So regeneration is a change in our nature while justification is a change in our standing before God. After we are born again, when we sin, we do not undo our regeneration or our justification, we do not lose our salvation, but we still have a need for further cleansing, and we receive such cleansing by confessing our sins to God.

We must confess, not cover our sin, and God will remove our sin from us as far as the east is from the west. We must stop covering, but we also need to change our hiding place.

THE NEED TO CHANGE YOUR
HIDING PLACE

In verse 7, David confesses that God has become his hiding place, and then God answers in verses 8 and 9: "I will instruct thee and teach thee in the way which thou shalt go: I will guide thee with mine eye. Be ye not as the horse, or as the mule, which have no understanding: whose mouth must be held in with bit and bridle."

God is speaking here, and, in the context, it's not general guidance He's giving. Rather, He counsels us to stop hiding and stop covering and come to Him freely. We are not to be like a horse or a mule which are only controlled by force.

My grandfather, whom we called Big Murray, was a professional cowboy. He and my grandmother lived in

---

13. James M. Renihan, ed., *A Baptist Catechism* (Escondido, CA: The Association of Reformed Baptist Churches, 2004), 12.

central Florida and I spent most of my summers there as a child. When I was six, Big Murray taught me how to ride a horse and I went with him on cattle drives. He had one horse that was so self-willed, we had to resort to using a hackamore on him. A hackamore is a bit which is broken and pinned in the middle and when you pull back on the bridle, it puts tremendous pressure and pain on the horse's lower jaw.

My other granddad, whom we called Dada, had mules. They farmed and logged with mules. Dada did not like for his boys to ride mules because he always said that you couldn't trust a mule. I guess my Dad and his brothers were about as stubborn as mules because they rode them anyway, especially my Uncle Henry. My dad tells the story of one mule in particular that was incredibly stubborn and who would hardly do anything without being given a sharp kick in the sides. They learned finally to go ahead and give this mule one big gut-busting kick in the side when they first got on him; then afterwards, he was just fine. He got over his stubbornness and would do whatever they wanted him to do.

When we become sensitive to the pleasure or displeasure of God, we don't need "hackamores" or "kicks in the side." The instruction of His Word and the work of His Spirit are enough. Psalm 32:8 tells us that God will guide us with His eye or His look. God communicates His look to us through a heart well trained by His Word and Spirit. We simply can't be like Jiminy the Cricket and "always let our conscience be our guide" because an untrained conscience is surely no safe guide. Our conscience must be informed by Word and Spirit.

Must God result to stern chastening to get your attention, or is He able to communicate His will by the gentle promptings of His Spirit and His Word? Do your responses to Him demonstrate that you still need a bit and bridle? Does He have to treat you like a stubborn old mule? If so, you're still covering. You're not yet finding Him to be your hiding place. You've not yet learned to rest in the confidence that your covenant Lord loves you with His unfailing covenant love, and that He has transferred your sin to Christ and clothed you in His righteousness.

By the Spirit's grace, learn the blessedness of living with your sin covered by Christ. Cease living in the presence of others and for others and you will be freed to live in the presence of a God whose love and justice meet in Christ. Get to know the blessedness of confessing your sin and finding your hiding place in God. Then, as the psalmist says, you shall be surrounded by mercy and songs of deliverance.

DISCUSS THE ISSUES

1. Why do we live in the presence of others and for others rather than live freely in the presence of God and for God? When we sin, why do we often act as if nothing at all has happened? What are the consequences of not guarding our imagination along with our heart?

2. Read 2 Samuel 12:1–10. How could David's anger be kindled so strongly against the man in Nathan's parable and not at all against his own sin? Why did Adam and Eve not hide before the Fall? What were their characteristic sins after the Fall? What are common ways in which you cover your sin? Do you seek to know your own heart well? Why or why not?

3. Define confession. Why may we never find peace with God or relief from our sin if we are unwilling to confess our sin? Why is it as important to confess the sinful condition of our heart as it is to confess committing acts of sin?

4. What is justification? How does justification differ from regeneration? Explain how living in the security of God's justifying grace is the answer for hiding our sin. What does it mean to find your hiding place in God? What is the point of using the horse and mule as illustrations in Psalm 32:9? How may we train our mind and heart to be sensitive to the pleasure and displeasure of God?

SOLVE THE SCENARIO

Ellie cleaned out Leonard's closet and decided to get rid of a stack of old magazines. When she asked Ray, their sixteen-year-old son, to take the magazines out to the trash bin, she didn't realize that there was a pornographic magazine tucked away in the middle. Thumbing through them on the way out to the trash bin in the garage, Ray came across the one tucked away in the middle. Engrossed in the magazine, Ray didn't hear his dad drive up until it was too late. Ray was caught, but now so was Leonard. Always managing somehow to hide his "secret sin" from Ellie, though not at all able to hide the effects of it, Leonard has struggled with and against pornography for a long, long time. In fact, the first pornographic magazine he ever saw at age fourteen belonged to his father. Leonard, Ellie, and Ray each profess faith in Christ. Also, Leonard has never shared his struggle with anyone, especially the men of his church.

Identify as many of Leonard's sins as you are able to, starting with his root sin. What must Leonard do to put his sin right with God, with his wife, and with his son? Outline the biblical process which Leonard must pursue in order to experience real and lasting change. Give reasons why you ordered the steps of the process as you did. Is there a need or even an obligation for Leonard to share his problem of pornography with the leadership and/or more mature men of his church? If so, what should their response be to Leonard? If Leonard is unwilling to go to the leadership, what responsibility do Ellie and Ray have to go to them? Ray has always wondered why he and his Dad have never had a healthy father and son relationship; now he knows. What should the leadership do to help Ray, now that he's been exposed to his dad's pornography, his hidden life, and the source of so much pain for the last sixteen years?

SIT AT THE FEET OF CHRIST-CENTERED, EXPERIENTIAL TEACHERS

The Enemy Within: Straight Talk About the Power of Defeat of Sin, by Kris Lundgaard (*Level:* Basic)

Overcoming Sin and Temptation: Three Classic Works by John Owen, edited by Kelly M. Kapic and Justin Taylor (*Level:* Intermediate)

On the Mortification of Sin; On Temptation; On Indwelling Sin in Believers, by John Owen (*Level:* Intermediate to Difficult)

"Contrition and Confession," chapter 3 in *Soul Heights and Soul Depths,* by Octavius Winslow (*Level:* Basic to Intermediate) http://www.gracegems.org/WINSLOW/Contrition%20and%20Confession.htm

Personal Declension and the Revival of Religion in the Soul, by Octavius Winslow (*Level:* Basic to Intermediate)

2 Corinthians 7

Having therefore these promises, dearly beloved, let us cleanse ourselves from all filthiness of the flesh and spirit, perfecting holiness in the fear of God. ²Recieve us; we have wronged no man, we have corrupted no man, we have defrauded no man. ³I speak not this to condemn you: for I have said before, that ye are in our hearts to die and live with you. ⁴Great is my boldness of speech toward you, great is my glorying of you: I am filled with comfort, I am exceeding joyful in all our tribulation. ⁵For, when we were come into Macedonia, our flesh had no rest, but we were troubled on every side; without were fightings, within were fears. ⁶Nevertheless God, that comforteth those that are cast down, comforted us by the coming of Titus; ⁷and not by his coming only, but by the consolation wherewith he was comforted in you, when he told us your earnest desire, your mourning, your fervent mind toward me; so that I rejoiced the more. ⁸For though I made you sorry with a letter, I do not repent, though I did repent: for I perceive that the same epistle hath made you sorry, though it were but for a season. ⁹Now I rejoice, not that ye were made sorry, but that ye sorrowed to repentance: for ye were made sorry after a godly manner, that ye might receive damage by us in nothing. ¹⁰For godly sorrow worketh repentance to salvation not to be repented of: but the sorrow of the world worketh death. ¹¹For behold this selfsame thing, that ye sorrowed after a godly sort, what carefulness it wrought in you, yea, what clearing of yourselves, yea, what indignation, yea, what fear, yea, what vehement desire, yea, what zeal, yea, what revenge! In all things ye have approved yourselves to be clear in this matter.

CHAPTER FOUR

The Grace of Repentance

————— ❧ —————

In John Bunyan's allegory *Pilgrim's Progress,* his characters
Interpreter and Christian come upon a man in a dark room
seated in an iron cage. From all appearances, the man is very
sad. He sits with his eyes staring at the ground and his hands
folded. He sighs as if his heart will break. So Christian asks,
"Who are you?" "I am what I once was not," the man
answers. "What were you before?" Christian responds. "At
one time I was a man who professed Christ, and in my own
eyes and the eyes of others my faith was pure and growing."
"Well, what are you now?" Christian asks. "I am now a man
of despair, and locked up in my despair as I am locked up in
this Iron Cage. And I cannot get out. I cannot!" "But how
did you get in this condition?" asks Christian. "I ceased to
watch and be sober. I allowed myself to be driven by my
lusts, and I sinned against the light of the Word of God and
the goodness of God. I have grieved the Holy Spirit, and
He is gone from me; I allowed an opening for the Devil,
and He has come to me; I have provoked God to anger, and
He has left me; I have so hardened my heart that I cannot
repent." "But must you be kept in this iron cage of despair?
Is there no hope?" Christian questions. "No, none at all," the
man says. "Why? The Son of the Blessed is very merciful."

"Because I have...despised His very person; I have despised His righteousness; I have counted His blood as an unholy thing; I have shown utter contempt for the Spirit of grace. Therefore, I have shut myself out from all the promises, and nothing remains for me but threatenings, dreadful threatenings, fearful threatenings of certain judgment and fiery wrath which will consume me as an adversary."

The illustration of the man locked up in the iron cage is a fitting image of those who are unable to repent because they "go on sinning willfully, after receiving the knowledge of the truth" (Heb. 10:26–31). It's one of the last images emblazoned upon Christian's mind before he sets off on his journey to the Celestial City. And as he leaves, Interpreter turns to Christian and says, "Remember this man's misery, and let it be a caution to you forever."[1]

In 2 Corinthians 7, Paul exhorts us to purify ourselves and to bring our holiness to its completion in the fear of God. And he does so in the context of describing true and false repentance. What is true repentance, and how may we know we possess the repentance which leads to life, and not to death? In this study I want us to look at the grace of repentance.

TRUE REPENTANCE: THE GOOD
END OF GODLY SORROW

Paul comments in verse 7 that his joy over the Corinthians was greater than ever before. Verses 8 through 11 give the reason. In verse 8, Paul refers to a difficult letter which caused him much pain to write, and which evidently

---

1. John Bunyan, *The Pilgrim's Progress*, ed. Cheryl Ford (Wheaton IL: Tyndale House, 1991), 32–34.

caused the believers at Corinth much pain to read. The members of the church at Corinth had been tolerating sin among themselves such as was not even practiced among unconverted people. First Corinthians 5 describes a young man living in incest with his father's wife. He had taken his stepmother as his own wife. Perhaps his father had died or perhaps his father and step-mother were divorced, but the specific details don't matter; sacred Scripture condemns any marriage at all between family relations. So Paul wrote to rebuke them severely, although it caused him great pain to do so. Paul was like a caring father who has verbally corrected his son, but his son disregards his father's correction and keeps right on disobeying. So the father has to take his son into another room and spank him. As this father applies the rod of correction, the son begins to cry. His father embraces him and holds him close and he cries also.

Did Paul regret reproving his beloved Corinthian friends? Does any good father regret spanking his children? The answer is both yes and no! A good father is sad that he has to resort to spanking his child and he is sad that he caused him pain, but a good father is also glad he spanked him because of the results it produced in him. Paul says in verse 9 that his severe reproof caused the Corinthians a kind of sorrow which led to their repentance. His reproof caused them much sorrow, yet it did them much good! God used Paul's correction to produce salvation which leads to life.

Pastoring and parenting are similar in many ways. Pastors and parents can under-correct and they can over-correct. They can also give comfort too soon and they can give comfort too late. However, the right balance of instruction in law and gospel and proper care and comfort is a great instrument in achieving good and godly ends.

George Whitefield was one of the greatest preachers who ever lived. He preached many times in the open air and crowds of ten to twenty thousand people would gather to hear him. He was from England and crossed the Atlantic many times to minister among the thirteen colonies during the mid-1700s. While in America, Whitefield once heard Gilbert Tennent preach, and he said that he had never heard such a searching sermon. He came to the conclusion that in his own preaching he had been "giving comfort too soon." If a preacher thinks that the most important aim in preaching is to have people accept his sermons, he is bound never to cause the kind of sorrow that turns people outside themselves and sets them searching for the source of true repentance.[2]

THE SOURCE OF TRUE REPENTANCE

In the last part of verse 9, Paul points to the source of true repentance. He writes literally, "for ye were made sorry after a godly manner." This indicates that the Corinthians experienced the promised grace of repentance. In the new covenant, God promises to take away indifferent, hard, stony hearts and to give hearts that hate sinful actions and sinful desires—*the source of sinful actions*. Ezekiel 36:31 attaches the strongest language possible to the promised grace of repentance. God there says He will give us a heart that remembers its evil ways and its evil deeds and that we will loathe ourselves because of our iniquity; we will see our least sin for what it really is—an abomination against God.[3]

---

2. Geoff Thomas, sermon manuscript on 2 Corinthians 7:8–11, www.alfredplacechurch.org.uk/
3. cf. Ezek. 36:22–32; 2 Tim. 2:24–25.

Our flesh cannot possibly pump repentance out of a heart that is indifferent to God's covenant graces. The flesh cannot possibly produce power to overcome even one single sin, but the covenant grace of God in the gospel can. Paul writes in Romans 2:4 that God's kindness is the grace that leads us to repentance. In Psalm 130:4, David says that God's forgiveness is the grace that leads us to live in penitential fear, reverence, and awe. That's why we can conclude with Paul that there is a kind of sorrow and repentance which leads to life, and a kind of sorrow and repentance which leads to death. Paul contrasts the two in verse 10.

TRUE AND FALSE
REPENTANCE CONTRASTED

In 2 Corinthians 7:10, the Holy Spirit says that "godly sorrow worketh repentance to salvation not to be repented of: but the sorrow of the world worketh death." There's a kind of sorrow for sin that has its source in the world; it is of the world. There's also a kind of sorrow that has its source in God; it is of God. In verse 10, Paul expresses two characteristics of the kind of sorrow for sin that has its source in God: regret and repentance. What's involved in the kind of repentance for which we never need have regret is a change of mindset (*metanoeo*), accompanied by a life-long moral and spiritual turnaround (*epistrepho*).[4] Real repentance involves turning from sin and turning to God. We must repent believingly and we must believe repentantly. Repentance and faith are two sides of the same coin.

---

4. Sinclair Ferguson, "Repentance, Recovery, and Confession," in *Here We Stand: A Call from Confessing Evangelicals,* ed. James M. Boice and Benjamin Sasse, (Grand Rapids: Baker Books, 1996), 133.

Shortly after 9/11, there were all kinds of conspiracy theories, and one of them involved folding a dollar bill to see the twin towers standing and the twin towers collapsed. (Some people have a lot to do in their spare time.) Another much older conspiracy theory involves the Illuminati, which is the pyramid with the single eyeball at the top on the back of a dollar bill. Now let's say that you like George Washington on your dollar bills, but you don't like the Illuminati. So you decide to make your own dollar bills and do away with the Illuminati. You wouldn't get very far before being put in jail for counterfeiting. The same is true of godly sorrow. It's a mere counterfeit without *both* repentance and faith.

There's a picture of true repentance in the parable of the prodigal son. Away from home, feeding on pig-slop, God awakens the prodigal to the true condition of his sinful heart. He gets up and retraces his every step back into the outstretched arms of a father who lavishes his love upon him. In the book of Jeremiah, God restores Israel from exile, but the people are not truly restored until they return to the land in which God has covenanted to fulfill His promise of blessing.[5] Sinclair Ferguson comments, "Biblical repentance is not merely possessing a sense of regret that leaves us where it found us. Biblical repentance is the radical reversal that takes us back along the path from which we have departed."[6]

There are other pictures of repentance equally as radical. In Jeremiah 4:4, repentance is the circumcision of the heart—the decisive, painful, and bloody act whereby we cut off our sin and drain all its lifeblood. In Hosea

5. Ibid.
6. Ibid.

10:12, repentance is the plowing up of the fallow ground of our hearts and minds until the Lord Himself rains down righteousness upon us. In Matthew 5:29–30, Jesus warned that it's better to go to heaven without a hand or an eye than to go to hell with both hands and both eyes.

Godly sorrow produces a repentance which leads to life, but worldly sorrow does not produce repentance. Instead, it produces a man-centered penance which leads to death. Worldly sorrow focuses on man's plans and man's schemes to live independently from God. Worldly sorrow always has its own ideas about how to get right with God, appease a guilty conscience, and put conflict right with others, but they are not God's ideas. As Jack Miller says, "A person with worldly sorrow is a preparationist: he or she is always getting ready for grace. The preparationist seeks to make himself worthy of grace so that God will reach out to him when once this work of preparation is completed."[7] The preparationist is self-deceived and cannot see that all he is doing is asking God to excuse sin and to "Christianize" an essentially lustful heart by making him a little more patient with others, or a little more tolerant. But God does not hear such prayers because in reality he is only asking God for help in order to live independently from God. Prayer for repentance is not a matter of intensifying your efforts in asking for help. In a very real sense, God does not even offer help. Rather, He offers Himself in your place and in the place of your natural abilities.[8]

The Bible gives many examples of people filled with self and worldly sorrow. Balaam desired to die like a righteous

---

7. C. John Miller, *Repentance and the 21ˢᵗ Century Man* (Fort Washington, PA: Christian Literature Publications, 2001), 19–20.
8. Ibid.

man, but he did not desire to live a righteous life (Num. 23:10). Esau cried buckets of tears, but he showed contempt for the covenant blessings of God because he could not endure an empty stomach for a single day (Heb. 12:16). Amnon mourned, but only because he could not satisfy his lusts. Therefore, he grieved himself sick until he defiled his half-sister Tamar (2 Sam. 13:2). Rehoboam was willing to reconcile with Jeroboam outwardly, but he never dealt with his hateful heart (1 Kings 14:30). Ahab mourned but also for the wrong reason. He couldn't have Naboth's vineyard. So he locked himself inside his bedroom and stopped eating until Jezebel told him how to rob Naboth of his vineyard; then he quickly "came to life" (1 Kings 21:4). Jehu had great zeal to rule over others, but none for God to rule over him. In the beginning of his reign, he was a good king, but in the end, his loyalty was divided (2 Kings 10:15–31). The rich young ruler was sorrowful, but only because he was unwilling to part with the riches upon which he had set his heart (Mark 10:17ff). Felix shook with fear when he saw himself condemned by God, but he would not put his adulterous heart right with Drusilla, her former husband, or with God (Acts 24:25). Felix had extensive knowledge about "the Way." He spoke often with Paul about faith in Christ, but he was self-deceived.

On their journey to the Celestial City in *Pilgrim's Progress,* Christian and Faithful meet a professing pilgrim whose name is Talkative. Christian knows him from the City of Destruction. He knows that Talkative will deceive almost anyone because he puts on his best image away from home, but at home his sinful, ugly heart shows its true colors. So Faithful asks Talkative a few straightforward questions to convince him of his sin, stop his mouth before God, and point him to the experience and power of saving grace.

The first question Faithful asks to confront Talkative's error is this: "How does the saving grace of God reveal itself when God is at work in a person's heart?" Talkative answers that where the grace of God is in the heart, it causes a great outcry against sin. Faithful points out that it's far different to cry out against sin than to hate one's own sin. The next question is, "What is the second thing by which you would prove a work of grace in the heart?" Quickly Talkative responds, "Great knowledge of gospel mysteries." Then Faithful says that this should have been the first sign, but first or last, it is also false, for knowledge, even great knowledge, may be obtained concerning the mysteries of the gospel, and yet there be no work of grace in the soul. "One kind of knowledge rests in mere speculation about religious things; the other is accompanied by faith and love that moves a person to do the will of God from the heart." "Saving grace," says Faithful, "brings conviction of sin, especially of the corruption of the old nature, and of the sin of unbelief for which he will surely be damned if he does not obtain mercy from God.... The experience of grace works a deep remorse and shame for sin in the heart and reveals the absolute necessity of agreeing with and submitting to Christ for salvation." Then Faithful puts a final question to Talkative: "Have you experienced this first work of grace? And does your religion stand on the power of word and tongue alone or on the power of actions and truth?"[9]

In his autobiography, the famed storyteller Mark Twain recalls many times he repented in his youth.

---

9. Bunyan, *The Pilgrim's Progress,* Ford, ed., 89–102.

Every time a tragedy struck my town, it would engulf me. My repentances were very real, very earnest; and after each tragedy they happened every night for a long time. But as a rule they could not stand the daylight. They faded out and shredded away and disappeared in the glad splendor of the sun. They were the creatures of fear and darkness, and they could not live out of their own place. The day gave me cheer and peace, and at night I repented again. In all my boyhood life I am not sure that I ever tried to lead a better life in the daytime.

He writes that the burning of Huck Finn in the village jail lay upon his conscience a hundred nights afterward and filled him with hideous dreams…in which

I saw his appealing face as I had seen it in the pathetic reality, pressed against the window-bars, with the red Hell glowing behind him…. The shooting down of poor old Smarr in Main Street at noonday supplied me with more dreams; and in them I always saw again the grotesque closing picture—the great family Bible spread open on the profane old man's breast by some thoughtful idiot, and rising and sinking to the labored breathings, and adding the torture of its leaden weight to the dying struggles…. In my nightmares I gasped and struggled for breath under the crush of that vast book for many a night as though I were in Smarr's place…. My teaching and training enabled me to see deeper into these tragedies than an ignorant person could have done. I knew what they were for. I tried to disguise it from myself, but down in the secret deeps of my heart I knew—and I *knew* that I knew. They were inventions of Providence to beguile me to a better life….There were awful nights, nights of despair, nights charged with the bitterness of death. After each tragedy I recognized the warning and repented; repented and begged; begged like a coward; begged like a dog. [10]

Mark Twain was certainly sensitive to his own moral depravity, but his reflections were nothing more than worldly sorrow. He was only sorry for himself, not sorry for sinning against a holy and loving God. Some recognize Twain's confessions as a thinly veiled criticism of God.

How about you? Do you agree with Christ and submit to Him regarding the absolute necessity of grace—not just to cover your guilt of sinning, but also to take away your inclination to sin? Do you look to Christ's work in the gospel for what Augustus Toplady calls the double cure—to save from wrath and make you pure—to cleanse you from the guilt of sin and its power?

In our woods, we have very succulent weed trees that grow like crazy. We have burned them, poisoned them, cut them down, pulled them out, and dug them up. For over ten years, we've gotten rid of every one in sight on our property, and every year new ones pop up. One recent morning while my wife Paula and I were running, I found what may be the parent tree putting out roots on our property and everyone else's in our neighborhood. It's about twelve inches in diameter and fifty feet tall. I hate the fact that every year I have to go and pull up more weed trees in our yard, but what I really hate is the fact that the parent tree was ever planted! Likewise, we must deal with parent sins—sins of the heart—the root sins which produce all our branch and

10. Charles Neider, ed., *Autobiography of Mark Twain* (New York: HarperCollins, 1959), 55–56; C. John Miller, *Repentance and the 21ˢᵗ Century Man,* 24–25.

leaf sins. Then and then only will we see the kind of fruits in keeping with repentance being produced in our lives.

THE FRUITS OF TRUE REPENTANCE

Regarding the fruits of true repentance, Paul writes, "For behold this thing, that ye sorrowed after a godly sort, what carefulness it wrought in you, yea, what clearing of yourselves, yea, what indignation, yea, what fear, yea, what vehement desire, yea, what zeal, yea, what revenge! In all things ye have approved yourselves to be clear in this matter" (2 Cor. 7:11).

Are you as earnest about the sinful condition of your heart as you are about your sinful actions? Do you possess an eagerness to be right with God and man? Is there indignation over the least sins in your life and are you alarmed that unrepentant sin is surely a sign that you may not possess the experience of saving grace in your heart at all?

The Bible requires us to change; unless we do, there's no hope for us. And there's not one single change from our sinful ways that is possible without repentance. God has appointed repentance as the means by which we grow in holiness and communion with God. In the first of his Ninety-Five Theses, Martin Luther wrote that "when Jesus said, 'Repent,' He meant that the whole of life of the faithful is to be an act of repentance."

At one o'clock on Friday, July 3, 1863, two signal guns sounded and a barrage of Confederate canon fire started outside Gettysburg, the likes of which no one had ever seen during the Civil War. It was the third day of the battle and the high water mark for the Confederacy. The fate of a nation rested on the results of that day. Fifteen thousand Confederate soldiers emerged slowly from the woods and a mile-wide group of men marched across an open field nearly a mile long. How ironic that Picket's charge began at Seminary Ridge and ended at Cemetery Ridge. There were 51,000 casualties in all at Gettysburg. Men's bodies were shattered to pieces by mini-balls, decimated by grapeshot, and dismembered and torn in two by cannonballs. Each one of them started well, and every one had all the good intentions of finishing well, but thousands upon thousands perished in the fight.

Will you allow your lack of repentance to be the cause of your soul perishing or the cause of being out of fellowship with God, your family, and your church family as David did for over a year? We cannot estimate the horror that one sin will cause in our own lives and in the lives of others. [11]

You may start well and have the best intention of finishing well, the best intention of being saved, the best intention of putting things right with God and with others, the best intention of repenting, the best intention of reading your Bible and praying through, but you have no idea the damage you will cause to your soul or to the soul of another person by committing the least sin. You may think you can control your sin, but you cannot! To justify a single sin is one of the most damning deeds you could ever do: one look at pornography, one lustful desire, one unlawful kiss or embrace, just a little immodesty intended to turn a man's head, one controlling or manipulative word, one angry word, one shady joke, one lie, one selfish act, one act of unbelief, one hint of coldness of heart that you do not hold in check, one bit of indifference to God. It sits there on your heart and it chokes the spiritual life right out of you. Then

---

11. Cf. Jeremiah Burroughs, *The Evil of Evils*.

you and those around you reap the consequences of it for the rest of your life and maybe theirs.

No sin is greater than God's forgiving grace, but we have no idea how one sin will dispose us to other sins for a lifetime of struggles. We simply cannot estimate the corrupting influence or the collateral damage of a single sin. Likewise, we simply cannot estimate the value of the warnings and appeals that God sends. Are you listening to God's warnings? Are you responding to His appeals? Or, are you neglecting His warnings? The warning to repent or perish is like a sign that says: *WARNING! BRIDGE OUT!* Will you keep traveling down the same road and neglect God's warnings to your own peril and the peril of those closest to you? God has been gracious to you by sending yet another warning. What will you do?

The work of the Spirit and the Word has exposed your heart to you. Will you continue in your sin? Or will you repent? What good do you imagine will come in waiting to repent? It will only harden you against God. Don't wait! Repent now! Why weary God with endless promises to repent like Felix before Paul in Acts 24, saying, "Tomorrow and tomorrow...," and tomorrow never comes? "The harvest is past," Jeremiah says, "the summer is ended, and we are not saved" (8:20). Today is the day of salvation; if you hear His voice, do not harden your heart (Heb. 4:7).

Do you hear His voice? If you hear the voice of God in the slightest degree of conviction or in the smallest tinge of conscience, then today is the day, and to wait is to harden your heart against God.

He offers a simple invitation. Whatever your sin, wherever you are in relation to God, repent! Repent and believe on the Lord Jesus Christ and you will be saved. The promise and the warning are clear: "Believe and be saved; believe not and be condemned." Then live a life, by the Spirit's grace, constant in faith and continual in repentance!

As long as you look within yourself for the source of strength to repent, you will know nothing of the source of strength in Christ. Cry out to God now and ask Him to grant a sorrow that brings repentance which leads to life and leaves no regret. Repent and enjoy a renewed relationship with God and with those around you.

DISCUSS THE ISSUES

1. Define repentance. Describe the differences between true and false repentance. List and describe the biblical metaphors for repentance.

2. Why do confessing and repenting of sinful actions without carefully considering and repenting of a sinful heart simply not go far enough? What is the difference between speculative knowledge of God and experiential knowledge? What are the preparationist's errors?

3. What is the evidence that searching prayer and searching preaching has penetrated the surface and gotten down into the recesses of our soul? What may happen when we are under conviction and spiritual duress and seek comfort too soon, or if we are counseling someone under conviction, and give comfort and consolation too soon? Using biblical examples of false repentance, describe the particular sin in which their false repentance resulted.

4. Discuss the damage caused by justifying a single sin. Is there any hope of change without repentance? Why or why not? What are the fruits of repentance?

SOLVE THE SCENARIO

John is the younger of two children. His father left home before he was born and he grew up with a domineering, over-protective mother, even though she tried to do her best. Because they felt sorry for him, John's mother and older sister always rescued him from any consequences of errors. This resulted in a number of besetting sins and weaknesses in his life while growing up, but because John was so gifted intellectually and socially, he was able to mask his faults fairly well. Now, after twenty years of marriage and raising three children of his own, John's besetting sins and weaknesses have begun to manifest themselves in very destructive ways for everyone in his path.

David, an elder at church, is as good a friend as John has ever allowed anyone to be. Late one afternoon, David dropped by to see John and confirmed his concern regarding the strained relationships in their home. For some time, David sensed that something was not quite right and tried to talk to him, but always smiling, John looked him squarely and steadily in the eyes and assured him that everything was fine. With heightened concern, David shared his observations at the elders' meeting on Tuesday evening, describing John's home as having a culture of self-pity and disrespect. The elders prayed fervently and agreed that one of them must go with David and confront John. John agreed to meet; David and his co-elder shared their observations and asked John what he'd like to do about putting everything right. Still not seeing the breadth or depth of his problems, or the consequences of not addressing them biblically, and yet smiling amiably, John responded, "Well, I guess I got a few loose lug nuts on this trailer I'm pulling, so to speak; I just need to stop the truck and tighten 'em up." More concerned than ever, David changed the analogy and said with great care, "John, I'm afraid you've been putting band-aids on cancer for a long time, and unless you're willing to stop shading the truth, put down your boxing gloves, and allow the leaders of the church to help you and your family, you're going to lose your family, your career, your ministry, and maybe even your soul." Like a bolt of lightning, the Holy Spirit awakened John to his sin; he began to weep and thanked the elders and especially David for pursuing him for so long. He agreed to stop shading the truth and to listen.

Try to put yourself in the elder's shoes and describe what John must do to restore his relationship with God and with his family, and to begin to develop healthy relationships of trust and care with the men in his life. If John had been unwilling to listen and receive the counsel of his elders, what would the elders have had to do?

SIT AT THE FEET OF CHRIST-CENTERED, EXPERIENTIAL TEACHERS

Repentance and the 21st Century Man, by C. John Miller (*Level:* Basic)

The Doctrine of Repentance, by Thomas Watson (*Level:* Basic to Intermediate)

"All of Life is Repentance," by Tim Keller (*Level:* Basic to Intermediate) *www.greentreewebster.org/Articles/ All%20of%20Life%20is%20Repentance.pdf*

"Repentance," by J. C. Ryle (*Level:* Basic to Intermediate) www.gracegems.org/24/Ryle_repentance.htm

Come Back, Barbara, by C. John Miller and Barbara Miller Juliani (*Level:* Basic)

Addictions, A Banquet in the Grave: Finding Hope in the Power of the Gospel, by Edward T. Welch (*Level:* Basic to Intermediate)

"Repentance Unto Life," by A. A. Hodge (*Level:* Intermediate) www.rtrc.net/documents/wcf/hodge/wcfaah15.htm

Psalm 19:12–14

Who can understand his errors? cleanse thou me from secret faults. [13]Keep back thy servant also from presumptuous sins; let them not have dominion over me: then shall I be upright, and I shall be innocent from the great transgression. [14]Let the words of my mouth, and the meditation of my heart, be acceptable in thy sight, O LORD, my strength, and my redeemer.

CHAPTER FIVE

Lord, Keep Me from All Sin, Especially from the Sin of Presumption

MEDITATION ONE

JUST AFTER CHRISTIAN'S burden is removed at the cross, he runs down the hill, unchained, eyes wide open, singing and leaping for joy. At the bottom of the hill he meets three pilgrims who are still chained and whose eyes are closed by sleep. What an incredibly amazing picture of contrast John Bunyan draws! The sight of the chained, sleeping pilgrims takes Christian completely by surprise, as it would any new believer. For a few moments, he stands intensely baffled because these three miserable men are not in the City of Destruction, nor are they in the Town of Stupidity, nor even outside the wall or outside the entry at the wicket gate. They are beyond the cross, inside the wall, and seemingly on the path to the Celestial City. Yet these three pilgrims remain chained and fast asleep. So Christian does what any healthy believer would do: he awakens and warns them. "Wake up and leave this place!" Christian cries. "Have a willing heart and I will help you out of your chains. If he who goes about like a roaring lion comes by, you will become his prey." Bunyan names these characters *Simple, Sloth,* and *Presumption.* Naively, Simple answers, "Danger? I don't see any danger." Sloth yawns and mumbles, "Just let me go back to sleep." And finally Presumption arrogantly asserts, "Every barrel must stand on its own." In other words, "I certainly don't need any help from you." So the three of them roll over and go back to sleep in their sin.

Psalm 19:12–13 climbs a scale of sins just as in the case of Bunyan's characters. Perhaps you've heard all your life as I have that all sins are equal in the eyes of God. But just because all sins will equally condemn a person does not mean that one sin is not greater than another.

Perhaps no passage helps us see this important distinction more clearly than Psalm 19:12–14. In verse 12, David asks, "Who can understand his errors?" Can you? Can I? Can anyone fully discern the sins of his own heart? Charles Spurgeon says of this question that it does not require interrogation, only exclamation! Everyone who has gazed intently into the perfections of God's holy law agrees wholeheartedly. There's no better place for a discovery of the glory of God's holiness and the darkness of our own sinfulness than Psalm 19 because of the marvelous descriptions it contains of the perfect law of the Lord. When the Spirit of God applies the law to our hearts, as Paul says in Romans 3:19–20 and 7:7–8, we gain a spiritual sense of our sin. So Spurgeon adds, "He best knows himself who best knows the Word of God."

David's question in verse 12 about knowing sins which seem out of sight is followed by the only appropriate response. God alone is able to acquit us of our hidden faults, for He alone knows them all and He alone has paid their just penalty. This in no way means that we neglect confession; 1 John 1:9

says that confession is God's appointed means of grace by which our sins are forgiven. However, it's a good thing that God's pardon is based on Christ's finished work and not our complete confession because we have sins that lay undetected even by the most mature believer. Spurgeon says, "The transgressions which we see and confess are but like the farmer's small samples which he brings to market, when he has left his granary full at home." Do you agree with Spurgeon? More importantly, do you agree with God? Do you see that there are hidden sins that lay upon our hearts undetected?

In verse 13, David offers an earnest prayer which we would do well to make our own. He says, "Keep back thy servant also from presumptuous sins; let them not have dominion over me: then shall I be upright, and I shall be innocent from the great transgression."

A godly person cries out for the Holy Spirit to keep him from all sin: sinful actions, sinful attitudes, sinful thoughts, and especially the sinful inclinations of his heart from which all sins have their source. The great joy of every true believer is to be kept back from both sinning and sinful inclinations. While the true believer knows that all sin hurts his growth, he is keenly aware that heart sins especially hinder his communion with God. However, when sin presents itself to a wicked person, he embraces it; he views sin as his friend, mocks the idea of sinfulness, and finds his best pleasure and comfort in it. But a righteous person considers sin his deadly enemy.

David regards sins of presumption to be at the top of the list of dangers. They are "great sins" which he desires never to overtake him.

Sinning presumptuously is to view grace as pardon only, and to assume that grace is always available to cover more sin. Presumptuous people may go to the cross to confess their sin, but they leave with no real intent to change—like the reprobate in Dante's *Inferno,* who, all the time he's repenting, has his eye on his next opportunity for sinning. Presumptuous sin is aggravated sin. It is sin piled on top of more sin. It is sin at the height of its dominion.

To divide sin into categories, as David does in verses 12 and 13, proves very helpful for the spiritually minded believer who desires to grow in the experience of grace, conformity to Christ, and communion with God. It offers tools for self-examination, conviction, confession, repentance, and recovery. If you carefully study the subject of sin, you will find that there are three categories of sins that correspond to the mind, affections, and will. David gives only two categories of sin here: sins of ignorance and sins of presumption. The third is the sins of weak-heartedness. It's not hard to see the progression or degree of darkness in each.

Paul's persecution of the church as an unregenerate man was a great sin, yet it was a *sin of ignorance.* Peter's denial of Christ was greater than Paul's persecution, yet his was the *sin of weak-heartedness.* Perhaps Peter's weak-heartedness is the reason for Jesus' probing questions and tests of love in his last recorded personal appearance to Peter in John 20. But David's murder of Uriah was far worse than the sin of Paul or Peter, because his was the *sin of presumption.* Paul says in 1 Timothy 1:13 that he persecuted the church out of ignorance. He thought he was doing right. Peter's denial was not done in ignorance; he knew very well that it was wrong to deny Christ before men and he had been forewarned. But, in the heat of the moment, his weak devotion prevailed over what he knew to be right. May we not deceive ourselves: our devotion is never greater than its active expression.[1]

But David's sin is another matter altogether. With Bathsheba, he erred in his judgment and gave in to the appetites and desires of his flesh. But his sin against Uriah was not a sin of the mind or of the affections only; his sin against Uriah was a sin of the will. David killed Uriah in cold blood. Lying awake at night, he thought of every plan he could to conceal his lust and adultery. Embittered by his unrepented, hidden sins, he deliberated; he plotted; he schemed, and he came to believe the lie that there was nothing to be done but to silence the man who tormented his conscience. He resolved that, no matter what the outcome of his sin, he would not have Uriah around. He simply would not face him. He could not! In his sinful condition, he was too weak, uncourageous, and irresponsible to do so. So he committed high treason against King Jesus and sinned presumptuously. His bitter envy dominated, proceeding from a perverse will that was hardened, not simply against Uriah, but against the love and grace of God. Presumptuous sins rise against every check of conscience or movement of the Spirit in our life. And how devastating it proves to be to our soul and everyone else involved. O Spirit of God, we beg Thee to keep us from presumptuous sins!

Three other corresponding categories may be helpful in self-examination to keep us from sinning presumptuously. They are coldness of heart, indifference, and hardness of heart. Whenever we feel the least coolness in our affections for God, whenever we turn to duty and not first of all to

---

1. Roland Allen, *Missionary Principles* (Grand Rapids: Eerdmans Publishing, 1964), 126.

love which is our primary motive and duty, whenever we
or someone else close to us sees in us the faintest results
of growing cold towards Christ—we must quickly return
to the cross of Christ. We must return to the place of our
first love, to the place of peace and rest and joy, to the place
where we first began our journey with Christ. If we go
anywhere else but to the cross, it will not fare well with us
because it indicates that we're trying to resolve our problem
on our own. We're trying to resolve it by some means other
than what God has appointed, and we will soon pass to the
stage of indifference to God. It is surely easier to confess and
correct at the first stage of cool affections towards Christ
and to fan the cooling embers of holy love into flames once
again. However, if we tolerate cool affections for any length
of time, it soon turns into indifference; and if we tolerate
indifference for any length of time, it soon turns into hard-
heartedness. Then it becomes so very difficult to confess
even the smallest and simplest sin.

Simple, Sloth, and Presumption did not heed Christian's
warnings. So, some time later, when Christiana and Great-
heart pass by the place where Christian had seen them
earlier, they do not see three sleeping, shackled sinners. A
little way off the other side of the path, with hands and feet
cuffed in chains, they find Simple, Sloth, and Presumption,
all hanging dead. These three had not come by way of the
cross after all, but like others before and after them, they
had climbed over the wall, as Jesus warned. The eyes of
their hearts had not been opened by the Spirit of God. They
had not entered through the wicket gate as Christian and
Christiana had. They had not passed beneath the cross. The
burden of their sin had not been taken away by the cross,
nor buried in the tomb with Christ. Nor had they with joy
unspeakable and full of glory sung the new song of God.

I don't know on what side of the wall or the wicket gate you stand. I don't know how you got where you are, but if you're not using the means of grace to confess your sin, repent, and restore your relationship with God, then you are prey for the one who goes about like a roaring lion seeking those whom he may devour.

Are there sins which you need to confess? Are there sins of simpleton dullness and ignorance? Is there slothful self-indulgence, or even prideful, willful presumption? Are there sins of thought, affection, and will from which you need to be cleansed and delivered? "Awake thou that sleepest, and arise from the dead, and Christ shall give thee light" (Eph. 5:14).

DISCUSS THE ISSUES

1. All sin is horrible evil, but why is it wrong to believe that no sin is greater than another in terms of its consequences in our lives? Why is it that "we know ourselves best when we best know the Word of God?" What are the hidden sins that easily lay upon our hearts undetected by us? What is the value of confessing sins which seem hidden to us? What encouragement may we draw from knowing that God forgives hidden faults when we ask Him?

2. How do unbelievers view sin? How should we as believers view sin? List various sins of the mind, the heart, and the will. Why is willful disobedience worse than sinning in ignorance or weakness? What contributes to coldness towards Christ? Describe how unrepentant sin at the level of cool or cold affections for God turns into indifference and how indifference turns into hardness of heart.

3. Why is it wrong to view grace as pardon only? Why may we not assume that grace is always available for forgiveness in sinning? Have you ever used the fall of great men of God like David to rationalize your sin or your lack of repentance? What will you do differently in order not to descend down the stairs of coldness and indifference, into the abyss of hard-heartedness?

SOLVE THE SCENARIO

After having been married for twenty years, sadly for everyone concerned, Jimmy committed adultery. Over the years, he had confided with his closest friend at church named Sam about his struggles with sexual temptation. However, Jimmy always regarded the greatest sin to be the outward act of adultery itself. So he went to the trouble of installing filters on all his televisions and computers, and even had his friend Sam put in the settings and passwords for further protection. During the summer, Jimmy's family loved going to the beach, but he took them to the mountains instead because he just couldn't handle the immodesty. Finally, Jimmy gave in to what his heart desired most. A long time before it ever happened, Sam could see it coming because he believed Jimmy was treating his problem in an outward, moralistic, man-centered manner. Sam agreed with Jimmy many times that the temptation to adultery is very strong for him also, especially as immodest as our culture is these days. Sam had urged him to consider more carefully that the real need is not conquering a few outward sins, but in becoming God-centered personally and in leading his family to do the same. Finally, broken over his sin against God, his wife, his children, his church, and even his adulteress and her family, Jimmy asked for help to put his sin right and to become a God-centered man, husband, father, church member, and friend.

Put yourself in Sam's place and map out the process for putting Jimmy's sin right, for having God's perspective on sinful actions, thoughts, attitudes, and inclinations of the heart, and finally in moving away from man-centeredness to become God-centered.

SIT AT THE FEET OF CHRIST-CENTERED, EXPERIENTIAL TEACHERS

Respectable Sins: Confronting the Sins We Tolerate, by Jerry Bridges (*Level:* Basic)

Keeping the Heart, by John Flavel (*Level:* Basic to Intermediate)

The Sinfulness of Sin, by Ralph Venning (*Level:* Intermediate)

The Evil of Evil, by Jeremiah Burroughs (*Level:* Intermediate to Difficult)

"What is Sin," in *The Journal of Biblical Counseling*, by David Pawlison (Spring 2007; Vol. 25, No. 2) pp. 25–26 (*Level:* Basic to Intermediate) http://www.monergism.com/what_is_sin_by_david_powlison.php

"The Sinfulness of Sin," thirteen-part mp3 series by John MacArthur Jr., www.traviscarden.com/resources/podcast-archives/grace-to-you/series/the-sinfulness-of-sin/

"The Deceptiveness of Sin," by Hans Madueme (*Level:* Basic) http://thegospelcoalition.org/articleprint.php?a=53

The Gospel for Real Life, by Jerry Bridges (*Level:* Basic)

God is the Gospel: Meditations on God's Love and the Gift of Himself, by John Piper (*Level:* Basic)

The Gospel Mystery of Sanctification, by Walter Marshall (*Level:* Intermediate)

Isaiah 59:1–2

Behold, the LORD'S hand is not shortened, that it cannot save; neither his ear heavy, that it cannot hear: ²But your iniquities have separated between you and your God, and your sins have hid his face from you, that he will not hear.

CHAPTER SIX

The Highest Motive of Repentance of All: Enjoying Restored Fellowship with God

MEDITATION TWO

SHORTLY AFTER CHRISTIAN meets the three sleeping pilgrims named Simple, Sloth, and Presumption, he sees two other men tumbling over the wall on the left side of the narrow way. They introduce themselves as Mr. Formality and Mr. Hypocrisy. Christian asks where they are from and where they are going. They say that they were born in the Land of Vain-Glory and are on their way to Mt. Zion to receive praise. Christian questions them about how they got on the Way, but they tell him not to worry—that what they did was a custom dating back for a thousand years and, except for the coat Christian wears to cover his shame and nakedness, there's no difference between them at all. They then seek to assure Christian that they would obey the laws of the Lord of the land just as conscientiously as he would. For a while they travel together along the Way until they come to the foot of Hill Difficulty. Christian refreshes himself in the stream of the Water of Life, and up he goes. But because the hill is so steep and so high, Formality and Hypocrisy take the two level paths of least resistance. Formality takes the path to the left called *Danger*, and it leads him into a giant forest never to be seen again. Hypocrisy takes the path to the right called *Destruction,* and it leads to a vast field full of dark mountains and there he stumbles, never to rise again.

Formality and hypocrisy kill grace and quench communion with God. Samuel Rutherford once said that you can paint a man, but not the soul of a man; and you can paint a fire, but not the heat of a fire; and you can paint a rose, but not the smell of a rose. Jim Elliot added, "Paint we have in abundance; power we lack."

Being free from formality and hypocrisy in our lives is extremely costly. It costs us the bloody and painful act of circumcising our hearts. It costs us the strain and toil of plowing up the fallow ground of our lives and it costs retracing every step we've taken away from home and the strong arms of our loving, heavenly Father. But such work is well worth all the effort.

The opening verses of Isaiah 59 offer the highest motive of all for the very necessary and very hard work of repentance: enjoying fellowship with God.

THE UNREPENTANT SINNER'S
ACCUSATIONS AGAINST GOD

Isaiah 58 describes the plight of a people who seem to be deserted by God and for whom the hoped-for promises of glory fail to materialize, so they accuse God of weakness and severity. They also cry out to God, but He just doesn't seem to be listening. Then God refutes their accusations of His powerlessness and the dullness of His hearing. The High King of Heaven says that He has as powerful a hand and as willing an ear as ever. The problem is not with God; the problem is with His people. He has not changed, nor does He change. But we have and we do. Next, in chapter 59, Isaiah reveals the unrepentant sinner's accusations against God, and then he explains why God hides His face and will not answer.

GOD'S EXPLANATION AS TO WHY HE HIDES HIS FACE AND WILL NOT ANSWER

Isaiah 59:2 offers three of the most awful results of unrepentant sin in the life of a professing believer. The first is that "our sin separates us from God." The second is that it "hides the face of God from us." Then thirdly, "God no longer hears our prayers." Separation from God manifests itself in many ways. Spiritual strength and vitality leave us so that we waste away. The peace of a clear conscience vanishes. With the life and vitality of our soul gone, God removes the light of His countenance; His glory departs, darkness descends, restlessness settles, and the look of death is displayed upon our face. We may cry out to God for help, but He will not answer. Why? Because our sins have hidden His face, dulled His ear, and stayed His hand. And in this condition, there's only one thing to do—forsake our sin because it is displeasing to God.

Enjoying the sweetness of felt communion with God is the highest motive for repentance. The more pleasure we derive from our communion with God, the stronger our desire for His fellowship will be and the more dissatisfied we are without it. The absence of communion with God will embitter every other pleasure in life. It's not unlike being in love with someone and having lost them; you lose interest in those things you loved to do together.

When my grandfather retired in the late 1960s, he moved to the country and built a house with a five-acre pond in front of it for my grandmother, just because my grandmother liked to fish. When the fish were biting well, they would go down to the pond together almost every afternoon. My Dada would bait my Granny's hook and take her fish off the line. All she had to do was catch fish, and how she loved it so. Dada enjoyed her pleasure in catching fish as much as he did in catching his own. Granny baked homemade buttermilk biscuits for Dada almost every meal just because he enjoyed biscuits with homemade cane syrup so much. But when Dada died in December of 1988, Granny stopped fishing and only rarely baked biscuits. Why? Because the one whom she loved being with most was gone!

Our absence of communion with God embitters every other pleasure because He created all pleasure for His glory and our joy in Him. Are you sensible to the presence or absence of communion with God? Are you aware when the fine edge of affection for God is dulled to any degree by your sin and, more specifically, your lack of faith in the attentiveness of God's ear or His strong arm of salvation? Are you deepening, increasing, and expanding your delight in God Himself by repenting when you sin? Or are you comfortable being separated from God, having Him withhold the light of His countenance from you, and not hearing your prayers? If you're not repenting, isn't the wall of separation between you and God high enough already? Why should you build the wall of separation higher by refusing to simply trust His goodness, confess your sin, and repent? Why should you be content without the sweetness of felt communion with God? There simply can be no fellowship with God at all when we remain in sin and unbelief.

Being free from formality and hypocrisy in our lives is very costly. It means decreasing in our own eyes and also decreasing in the eyes of others. It means slaying the dragons of outward performance and appearances. It means clearing our minds of small thoughts of God, ridding our hearts of small affections for God, and filling our minds and hearts with God's greatness. It means fighting the fight of faith against everything that militates against true faith. It means paying attention to the true condition of our soul and taking personal ownership of the underlying root causes. It means grieving over our sins and the sinfulness of our condition. It means not shifting blame to anyone or anything else. And it means simple, heartfelt, straightforward confession of sin and repentance. Yes, being free from formality and hypocrisy is very costly, but it is well worth it all. May we grow in personal repentance of daily sins in order to enjoy restored communion with God.

DISCUSS THE ISSUES

1. Are Mr. Formality and Mr. Hypocrisy right to think that the only thing that causes them to differ from Christian is the coat he wears to cover his shame and nakedness? Is this difference that important? Why or why not? Why are formality and hypocrisy such grace killers?

2. In what ways do we show that we believe the problem lies with God's weakness or His inability to hear rather than with us?

3. List and discuss the results of the lack of repentance. List and discuss various motives for repentance. Why is fellowship with God the highest motive? What keeps us from knowing, believing, and feeling that the "High King of Heaven has as powerful a hand and as willing an ear as ever"?

4. Why does the absence of communion with God embitter ever other pleasure that we may experience in life? Are there sins you need to repent of, and what costs do you need to pay in order to repent your way back to God? Do you believe that these costs are worth paying? What measures will you take to be free from formality and hypocrisy?

SOLVE THE SCENARIO

Five years ago, Jerry, Jan, and their daughter Anna moved next door. Jerry and Jan profess faith in Christ and occasionally attended church before they made the move, but, as long as you've known them, they've not attended. You've sought to engage them many times on a spiritual level, but they've never shown any significant interest. Recently, fifteen-year-old Anna has become quite interested in a young man at school named James who expresses no interest in God or spiritual things, leads a very aimless life, and uses drugs. When Jerry and Jan first discovered Anna's interest in James, they asked her not to see him any longer. Then they found out that not only had Anna disregarded their request, but Anna has been very inappropriately involved with James physically. Even though Anna's parents forbid her to have any contact at all with James, she continues to meet him secretly after school. Jerry and Jan have talked and even pled with her many times, but to no avail. They explain that sex outside marriage is morally wrong and tell her what a loser James seems to be; they reason that she's a very bright girl with a great future and she doesn't need to throw her life away by getting pregnant or by hanging around a dull guy with such questionable character. When they talk, Anna simply clams up and won't discuss anything with her parents at all. The more Jerry and Jan talk, the more Anna distances herself from her parents relationally.

You've sought to build a good relationship with Jerry, Jan, and Anna to engage them spiritually and have prayed diligently for them. Now Jerry and Jan come to you and share their struggles. They ask lots of questions about how you've kept up such a close relationship with your kids through their teenage and college years and how you motivated them to stay morally pure, and they are even expressing an interest in your relationship with God. God seems to have opened the door for you to serve your neighbors in a big way. What counsel will you give about how to recover their relationship with Anna and steer her in a better course morally?

SIT AT THE FEET OF CHRIST-CENTERED, EXPERIENTIAL TEACHERS

God is the Gospel, by John Piper (*Level:* Basic)

The Pleasures of God: Meditations on God's Delight in Being God, by John Piper (*Level:* Basic to Intermediate)

God's Passion for His Glory, edited by John Piper (*Level:* The first half of the book by John is Basic to Intermediate; the second half entitled *A Dissertation on the End for Which God Created the World,* by Jonathan Edwards, is Intermediate to Difficult.)

The Glory of the Redeemer, by Octavius Winslow (*Level:* Intermediate) http://gracegems.org/W/glory.htm

"Love Christ Because of His Glory," by Thomas Shepard (*Level:* Basic to Intermediate), www.puritansermons. com/shepard/sheprd10.htm

"The Divine Glory of Christ," four sermons on mp3 by Geoff Thomas, www.alfredplacechurch.org.uk/ sermons/#Glory

"The Glory of God," a sermon on mp3 by Dr. D. Martyn Lloyd Jones, http://berbc.org/onlinesermons/Dr%20 Martyn%20Lloyd%20Jones/LJ05_GloryOfGod.mp3

2 Corinthians 4:7

But we have this treasure in earthen vessels [these jars of clay], that the excellency of the power may be of God, and not of us.

2 Corinthians 7:5–10

For, when we were come into Macedonia, our flesh had no rest, but we were troubled on every side; without were fightings, within were fears. ⁶Nevertheless God, that comforteth those that are cast down, comforted us by the coming of Titus; ⁷and not by his coming only, but by the consolation wherewith he was comforted in you, when he told us your earnest desire, your mourning, your fervent mind toward me; so that I rejoiced the more. ⁸For though I made you sorry with a letter, I do not repent, though I did repent: for I perceive that the same epistle hath made you sorry, though it were but for a season. ⁹Now I rejoice, not that ye were made sorry, but that ye sorrowed to repentance: for ye were made sorry after a godly manner, that ye might receive damage by us in nothing. ¹⁰For godly sorrow worketh repentance to salvation not to be repented of: but the sorrow of the world worketh death.

CHAPTER SEVEN

Sorrow Over Sin for the Glory of Christ—The Price of Brokenness

MEDITATION THREE

WITH THREE HUNDRED MEN who lapped water like dogs, God promised to deliver an army of idolatrous Midianites into Gideon's hands. Every boy in the world would have loved to take part in the adventure of God's army on that great night. At the beginning of the second watch, Gideon and his men crept up on the outskirts of the camp of the enemy of God. Gideon's weapons of choice were much different from most soldiers' weapons. He had armed all his men with trumpets and clay pots. Underneath their clay pots they concealed their torches and on Gideon's signal each man broke his pot, let his light shine, blew his trumpet, and shouted, "The sword of the LORD, and of Gideon." And when they did everything God told them to do, their enemies fled in fear of a surprise attack from the army of God. Surely Paul has the story of Gideon in his mind when he writes in 2 Corinthians 4:7, "But we have this treasure in earthen vessels [these jars of clay], that the excellency of the power may be of God, and not of us."

We are the earthen vessels! We're the clay pots! The treasure we possess in our clay pots is the light of the knowledge of the glory of God shining in the face of Jesus Christ. And what is the price of the light of God's glory shining in your life? According to the first seven chapters of 2 Corinthians, it's the price of a broken vessel!

In the year 56 A.D., on his third missionary journey, Paul writes the letter of 2 Corinthians. In verse 5 of the seventh chapter, he says that he and the other missionaries with him experienced hardship at every turn in Macedonia and, most likely, in the city of Philippi, from which he is writing. Indeed, Paul says in 2 Corinthians 1:8, they were so utterly burdened beyond their strength that they despaired of life itself. In chapter 4, he describes them as being "troubled on every side, yet not distressed; we are perplexed, but not in despair; persecuted, but not forsaken; cast down, but not destroyed." In chapter 6, he adds that they endured troubles, hardships, distresses, beatings, imprisonments, riots, hard work, sleepless nights, and hunger. However, Paul says with resonating voice in 2 Corinthians 7:6: "Nevertheless God, that comforteth those that are cast down, comforted us." The word he uses for *cast down* means to be lowly—to be broken-hearted. God comforts humble, lowly, broken people. In chapters 1 through 7, there are many hurting and broken believers. Paul was broken, his fellow missionaries were broken, the Corinthian believers themselves were broken. In fact, the news Titus brings of the Corinthians' brokenness causes Paul great joy. The servant of God is happiest when he or she and those whom they are serving experience true brokenness. The price of God's glory shining in our lives is brokenness. Is that your experience? Does brokenness bring you joy?

Verse 10 describes two kinds of brokenness. One results from godly sorrow, the other from worldly sorrow. We know the difference between the two by the company they keep. Verse 10 says that godly sorrow produces repentance that leads to life, but worldly sorrow produces death. Worldly sorrow hardens our hearts against God and drives us away from God; godly sorrow softens our hearts and draws us near God. Paul says at the beginning of chapter 7 that we are to cleanse ourselves from all defilement "by perfecting holiness in the fear of God." When we fear God and place His honor above everything else, we become increasingly indignant about everything in our lives that does not result in the love of God and the glory of God. We become increasingly shamed that we would place the love of self above the love of God. And our hearts are broken each time we discover that we have dishonored God or in some way disbelieved that God loves us or have not lived in the light of His great love.

Godly sorrow not only leads us to open our hearts to God, it also leads us to open our hearts to others. In 2 Corinthians 6:11, Paul says that his heart is opened wide towards the Corinthians. The grace of God had come to him and caused him to be a worker for their joy, he tells us in 2 Corinthians 1:24. But he explains further in 6:12 that their hearts were restricted towards him. The grace of God had come to them in vain and their affections and the works of love it produced in them were very small and dried up. We simply cannot open our hearts wide towards one another if we're unwilling for our hearts to be broken. In the last chapter of C. S. Lewis' book, *The Four Loves*, entitled "Charity," he says,

To love at all is to be vulnerable. Love anything, and

your heart will certainly be wrung and possibly broken. If you want to make sure of keeping it intact, you
must give your heart to no one, not even to an animal.
Wrap it carefully round with hobbies and little luxuries;
avoid all entanglements; lock it up safe in the coffin of
your selfishness. But in that casket—safe, dark, mo-
tionless, airless…it will not be broken; it will become
unbreakable, impenetrable, irredeemable…. The only
safe place outside Heaven where you can be perfectly
safe from all the dangers of love…is Hell.[1]

The most awful experience of hell is that the light of the
glory of God will not be there. Nor will brokenness over sin,
or the love and openness of heart which brokenness produces, because the price is much too high for those who will
not repent. If we refuse to be broken over our sin and refuse
to die to self to which Christ calls us and in its place we
promote self, which is the inevitable result of refusing to be
broken over sin—then the glory of Christ and all He accomplished for us will become increasingly unimportant to us.
Selfish interest, selfish honor, and selfish glory will be more
compelling than our interest in Christ or His glory shining
in our lives. Brokenness causes us to open our hearts to God
and to others. If your heart is not open to love others and do
good to them—the best good—then you lack one of two
things: either you lack sufficient brokenness or a sufficient
motive for it. In either case, you must beg God for the desire
for His light to shine in your life above everything else.

What is the price of brokenness? It is this treasure in
earthen vessels—the light of the knowledge of the glory of

1. C. S. Lewis, *The Four Loves* (New York: A Harvest Book, 1960),
121.

God shining in the face of Jesus Christ. But the vessel must be broken for the light to shine! Will you pursue brokenness over your sin?

DISCUSS THE ISSUES

1. What is the difference between a hurting person and a broken person? Why does God comfort the broken but not the hurting? How may we know we are seeking for God to comfort us when we are hurting but not broken?

2. Describe a restricted heart. Describe a heart opened wide with the love of God in Christ. Do you agree with C. S. Lewis that "the only safe place outside Heaven where you can be perfectly safe from all the dangers of love…is Hell"? Why or why not? Are there areas in your life in which you are unwilling to be vulnerable to receive and show love to the people whom God has placed in your life? What is hindering you?

3. Motive is "almost everything" in the Christian life, but God can provide us with the most compelling of all motives—the love of God in Christ—and yet, we still can live a self-centered life. What must we believe and what must we do in order to live a humble, holy, and happy God-centered life?

SOLVE THE SCENARIO

James grew up in a highly dysfunctional home. His dad was hardly ever around because he worked so much, and when he was around, he had unreasonable expectations for James and often showed extreme disappointment when James didn't measure up. Therefore, James and his father have never been very close. James was converted during his sophomore year of college, but even after he became a Christian, he struggled with melancholy and didn't have any close friends because of his fears of being hurt. He's an amazingly gifted musician, writes poetry, and composes music. However, James has often been disappointed with himself because of his exceedingly high personal expectations. He's married to Cindy and they have an only child named Jimmy who just turned fifteen. James loves Cindy and Jimmy more than anything in the world; they have as good a family relationship as they possibly can, considering James' melancholic perfectionism and his often debilitating depression. This past year, James became so depressed, he quit his job and now remains in seclusion at home while Cindy works.

You're an old friend from the college ministry through which James came to Christ. You reached out to him during a time a crisis and you're probably the closest male friend he's ever had. Six months ago, you and your family moved to a city near James and Cindy and you decided to call. But it was at James' lowest point and he couldn't talk to anyone at the time. Yesterday, James called to ask you for help. He's the healthiest he's been emotionally in a long time, but James still has a long way to go in developing normal give and take relationships with others. Outline the process of growth in the experience of grace to help James and his family, especially being careful to include James' view of God, his view of himself, and his fears of being hurt.

SIT AT THE FEET OF CHRIST-CENTERED, EXPERIENTIAL TEACHERS

Trusting God: Even When Life Hurts, by Jerry Bridges (*Level:* Basic to Intermediate)

"Trusting God: Even When Life Hurts," four mp3 messages by Jerry Bridges, http://www.graceaudio. org/archive.htm

"The Broken and Contrite Heart," chapter 5 in *The Inner Life,* by Octavius Winslow (*Level:* Basic to Intermediate) *http://gracegems.org/WINSLOW/The%20Broken%20and %20Contrite%20Heart.htm*

"All the Good that is Ours in Christ: Seeing God's Gracious Hand in the Hurts Others Do Us," a message given at the 2005 Desiring God Conference by Mark Talbot, http://www.desiringgod.org/media/audio/ conferences/national2005/2005.10.08_talbot_32k.mp3

"Making All Things New: Restoring Pure Joy to the Sexually Broken," an mp3 message by David Powlison, *www.desiringgod.org/media/audio/conferences/ national2004/10_20040925_powilson.mp3*

"Curse or Consecrate: Two Ways for a Christian to View a Conflict," by Ken Sande (*Level:* Basic to Intermediate) *http://www.peacemaker.net/site/c.aqKFLTOBIpH/ b.1084263/apps/nl/content3.asp?content_id={0285AEC9-A85D-4F16-95D8-A4AB8A5BB3C5}&notoc=1*

"Polemic Theology: How to Deal with Those who Differ from Us," by Roger Nicole, http://www.peacemaker. net/site/c.aqKFLTOBIpH/b.1084263/apps/nl/ content3.asp?content_id={12F7DAA8-63AE-4BEA-B210-EB548976264C}&notoc=1

"When I Fall, I Will Rise: Bold Brokenness," by John Piper www.desiringgod.org/ResourceLibrary/Sermons/ ByDate/1988/643_When_I_Fall_I_Will_Rise/

Acts 3:19

Repent ye therefore, and be converted, that your sins may be blotted out, when the times of refreshing shall come from the presence of the Lord.

Hosea 10:12

Sow to yourselves in righteousness, reap in mercy; break up your fallow ground [repent]: for it is time to seek the LORD, till he come and rain righteousness upon you.

CHAPTER EIGHT

How to Repent
of Daily Sins

GUIDE ONE

REMAINING SIN is a present reality in the life of every believer as the Holy Spirit so clearly teaches in Romans 7; therefore, Proverbs 28:13 warns, "He that covereth his sins shall not prosper: but whoso confesseth and forsaketh them shall have mercy." The great old catechisms of the past define repentance as a saving grace by which a sinner, out of a true sense of his sin and apprehension of the mercy of God in Christ, does, with grief and hatred of his sin, turn from it to God, with full purpose of and endeavor after new obedience. The issue we want to take up here is how we experience this grace.

I. THE MOTIVE OF REPENTANCE: TO ENJOY UNBROKEN FELLOWSHIP WITH GOD

> "Behold, the Lord's hand is not shortened, that it cannot save; neither his ear heavy, that it cannot hear: ²But your iniquities have separated you from your God, and your sins have hid his face from you, that he will not hear" (Isa. 59:1–2).

II. THE GROUND OR BASIS OF REPENTANCE: THE FINISHED WORK OF CHRIST

- Hebrews 10:1–23
- Romans 7:25–8:5

III. ELEMENTS OF REPENTANCE: THE RESTORATION OF FELLOWSHIP WITH GOD

A. Recognize that all sin is against God (Gen. 39:9; Ps. 51:4; Luke 15:18, 21). All sin causes us to be unlike God as well as contrary to God. Every sin is an act of rebellion, hostility, and enmity against Him. Sin is contrary to the nature of God and the will of God, and it's contrary to the gospel. It manifests itself as disagreeable to God and as ingratitude for God and His great remedy for sin in the Son of His love. Sin hinders communion with God and with the people of God.

B. Recognize the shamefulness and sinfulness of sin (Rom. 6:21; Ps. 51:1–17).

C. Confess the guilt of your sin (Rom. 3:19; 1 John 1:9).

D. Seek to fill your heart with sorrow and grief for your sin (2 Cor. 7:10).

E. Hate your sin because you know that it's displeasing to God and forsake it (Ezek. 36:31). View your sin as a most deadly evil.

F. Trust fully in the pardon of Christ and treasure the forgiveness of sin and the restoration of fellowship because of what Christ has done (Rom. 4:25–5:11). Repentance is not penance. We do not pay for sin; in fact, we cannot pay for sin. Once pardoned by the blood of Christ and clothed in His righteousness, God does not require further payment from us; but He does require repentance.

G. If needed, seek restoration and make restitution for sins committed against others (Matt. 5:23–24), but do not confuse this as earning God's forgiveness.

Isaiah 55:6–12

Seek ye the LORD while he may be found, call ye upon him while he is near: [7]Let the wicked forsake his way, and the unrighteous man his thoughts: and let him return (repent) unto the LORD, and he will have mercy upon him; and to our God, for he will abundantly pardon. [8]For my thoughts are not your thoughts, neither are your ways my ways, saith the LORD. [9]For as the heavens are higher than the earth, so are my ways higher than your ways, and my thoughts than your thoughts. [10]For as the rain cometh down, and the snow from heaven, and returneth not thither, but watereth the earth, and maketh it bring forth and bud, that it may give seed to the sower, and bread to the eater: [11]So shall my word be that goeth forth out of my mouth: it shall not return unto me void, but it shall accomplish that which I please, and it shall prosper in the thing whereto I sent it. [12]For ye shall go out with joy, and be led forth with peace: the mountains and the hills shall break forth before you into singing, and all the trees of the field shall clap their hands.

CHAPTER NINE

A Catalogue of Sins Seldom Confessed or Repented Of

GUIDE TWO

IN HIS LITTLE BOOK, *Words to Winners of Souls,* Horatius Bonar writes,

> In the year 1651 the Church of Scotland, feeling in regard to her ministers "how deep their hand was in transgression, and that ministers had no small accession to the drawing on of the judgments that were upon the land," drew up what they called a humble acknowledgment of the sins of the ministry.[1]

This document is a striking and searching one. It is perhaps one of the fullest, most faithful, and most impartial confessions of ministerial sin ever made." I have drawn upon their work in cataloging various sins which we as Christians frequently commit, and I encourage you to add particular sins which you commit and of which you need to confess and repent.

---

1. Horatius Bonar, *Words to Winners of Souls* (Phillipsburg, NJ: Presbyterian and Reformed Publishing, 1995), 25.

I. SINS RELATED TO NOT ORDERING MY LIFE ACCORDING TO THE GOSPEL:

- acting from, to, and for ourselves, rather than from, to, and for God;
- not seeking the practical knowledge and experience of the mystery of the gospel;
- not daily seeking a greater apprehension of the greatness of the gospel and of God;
- seeking a name for self rather than the honor of Christ;
- great inconsistency in our walk with God;
- instability and wavering in the ways of God;
- neglect of acknowledging God in all our ways;
- trusting in natural abilities or past successes rather than depending upon the Spirit;
- not esteeming the cross of Christ and sufferings for His name;
- fears of persecutions, hazard, loss of esteem, and the fear of man;
- practical legalism—offering fleshly, dutiful, legal obedience rather than gospel obedience, that is, the obedience that comes from faith in Christ;
- slighting fellowship with those from whom we might spiritually profit;
- not preaching the gospel to myself daily nor taking delight in it for my own holiness.

II. SINS RELATED TO NOT FEEDING MY SOUL DEVOTIONALLY:

- ignorance of God, His holy character, and His holy and just ways;
- lack of nearness with God the Father, God the Son, and God the Holy Spirit;

- taking little delight in those things which influence our communion with God;
- not studying to be complete in Christ;
- studying more to learn the language of holiness than the exercise of holiness;
- not improving prayer and fellowship with God and not mourning over these neglects;
- great selfishness in all that we do;
- seldom in secret prayer with God, except to fit ourselves for public performance;
- only reading the Scriptures in so far as it may fit us for our public ministry;
- glad to find excuses for the neglect of spiritual disciplines and duties;
- great neglect of reading the Scriptures and other good Christian literature;
- reading books and magazines which hinder my communion with God;
- using entertainment that hinders my communion with God;
- neglecting the reading of Scriptures in secret, for edifying ourselves as Christians;
- taking up little of God by reading good books, meditating, and speaking of God;
- speaking of Christ more by hearsay than from personal knowledge and experience.

III. SINS RELATED TO NOT ACTIVELY PUTTING REMAINING SIN TO DEATH:

- negligence in entertaining a sense of sin's guilt, misery, tyranny, and corrupting influences;
- not given to reflect upon our own ways;
- not allowing conviction to have a thorough work upon us;

- not watching over my heart nor the things my mind most often goes to when in neutral;
- not wrestling against corruption, nor studying mortification;
- not studying self-denial, nor resolving to take up the cross of Christ;
- seeking our own pleasure when the Lord calls for self-denial;
- not guarding nor wrestling against all seen and known evils, especially our besetting sins;
- little conscience made of secret humiliation and fasting;
- least careful of those things which are most remote from the eyes of others;
- being satisfied to outwardly restrain ourselves from sin as any moral unbeliever might;
- not being constrained inwardly by redeeming and re-newing grace to walk in holiness;
- not mourning for our own and other's guiltiness and great backslidings;
- foolish jesting away of time with impertinent and use-less talk;
- abusing time in frequent recreation and pastimes and loving our pleasures more than God;
- taking little or no time to participate in edifying conversation;
- hasty anger and passion in our families or with others;
- covetousness, worldly mindedness, and an inordinate desire after the things of this life;
- being taken up for the most part with the things of the world;
- artificial confessing of sin without repentance;
- professing to declare iniquity and not resolving to be sorry for sin;

- confession in secret much slighted, even of those things in which we are convicted;
- no reformation of life after solemn acknowledgments and private vows;
- more ready to search and censure faults in others than to see or deal with them in ourselves;
- not fearing to meet trials, but presuming in our own strength to go through them unshaken;
- not learning the fear of God when others fall into sin, nor mourning and praying for them;
- too much eyeing our own credit and applause;
- apathy and deadness of spirit.

IV. SINS RELATED TO THE MISUSE OF THE LORD'S DAY:

- neglecting the preparation of my heart and mind for the Lord's Day;
- not praying for the conscious smile of God or the sacred anointing upon my pastor;
- not praying for fellow Christians' spiritual benefit on the Lord's Day;
- common and ordinary discourse on the Lord's Day;
- neglect of engaging others in conversation in the things of the Lord;
- using the Lord's day for recreation and entertainment;
- not using the Lord's day for worshiping God and doing good to others;
- not taking to heart sermons or thinking on them with due care;
- slighting pastoral admonition from the Lord's Day sermon;

- not being careful to bring home the point by application to my soul as to find out the doctrine.

V. SINS RELATED TO NOT CARING FOR THE SOULS OF OTHER BELIEVERS:

- not taking measures to lead or order our family spiritually;
- negligent or inconsistent in daily family worship;
- not caring how unfaithful and negligent others are;
- being content with, if not rejoicing at, other's faults;
- not laying to heart the sad and heavy sufferings of the people of God abroad,
- not studying opportunities of doing good to others;
- preferring that our pastor or others admonish fellow Christians who are caught in sin;
- lightness and profanity in conversation unsuitable to a holy calling;
- carnal familiarity with natural, wicked men, so that we and they become hardened to their sin and our need to speak to them of turning from the wrath to come;
- conversing ordinarily with others for the worse rather than for the better;
- not praying for men of a contrary judgment, but using reservation and distance from them, being more ready to speak against them than to them or to God for them;
- not weighed with the failings of others;
- talking of and sporting at the faults of others, rather than showing them compassion;
- not cherishing godliness in God's people or praying for it;
- quenching the work of the Spirit in others by my neglect to minister to them;

- praying little for a work of the Spirit in my life and the lives of others;
- want of hospitality and charity to the members of Christ;
- not knowing how to speak a word in season to the weary;
- being lazy and negligent in the work of catechizing.

VI. SINS RELATED TO NOT PARTICIPATING IN THE PROGRESS OF THE GOSPEL:

- neglecting to fit ourselves for the progress of the gospel;
- not being concerned that the kingdom of Jesus Christ is not thriving;
- not rejoicing at the conversion of sinners;
- being content with the Lord's work not thriving among His people;
- spiritual purposes often dying in our hands when they are begun by others;
- not praying for the work of the revival of true religion;
- neglect of faithful prayer for the lost in my community and neighborhood;
- neglect in proclaiming the law and the gospel to unbelievers and believers alike;
- neglect in praying for pastors and missionaries.

John 15:5−8

I am the vine, ye are the branches: He that abideth in me, and I in him, the same bringeth forth much fruit: for without me ye can do nothing. [6]If a man abide not in me, he is cast forth as a branch, and is withered; and men gather them, and cast them into the fire, and they are burned. [7]If ye abide in me, and my words abide in you, ye shall ask what ye will, and it shall be done unto you. [8]Herein is my Father glorified, that ye bear much fruit; so shall ye be my disciples.

CHAPTER TEN

The Grace of Prayer

IN ONE OF CHARLES SCHULZ'S vintage *Peanuts* clips, Linus is kneeling by his bed in prayer and in walks Lucy. Linus says, "Lucy, I think I've made a new theological discovery!" "What is it?" she asks. Linus replies, "If you hold your hands upside down, you get the opposite of what you pray for."

Throughout church history, people have differed on the relationship of body posture and prayer. Should we pray with our hands open or folded, up or down? Sitting down or lying down? Standing or kneeling? Head covered or uncovered? Whenever Christians have thought carefully about the posture of the body in prayer, they have always concluded that body posture is not nearly as important as the posture, inclination, and attitude of our soul before God.

Even though I do not live under a monarchy, I have always known that it is right to bow in the presence of royalty. Philippians 2:10 says that there's a time coming when every knee shall bow and every tongue shall confess to the glory of God the Father that Jesus Christ is Lord. But what will it profit us, if we bow our knees and miss the beauty and glory of God revealed in the face of Jesus Christ?

When the fire of God fell on Mt. Carmel, Ahab went down to eat and drink; Elijah went up to pray, and the hand of God was upon Elijah (1 Kings 18:42). James tells us that Elijah was just a man with a nature like ours, but he prevailed in prayer, and God answered.

WHAT IS PRAYER?

Essentially, prayer is asking for something from God. It's making requests of God. In the late 1800's, D. L. Moody traveled through Scotland preaching a series of evangelistic conferences.[1] One afternoon he was asked to speak to hundreds of school children, and he thought to himself, "What should I talk to all these school children about?" The idea came to him to speak on prayer. So he began his message as preachers sometimes do with a rhetorical question. "What is prayer?" he asked. To his utter amazement, five hundred kids raised their hands. He was so stunned that at first he did not know what to think or do. So he decided to call on one of the boys down front, and he said, "Okay, what is prayer?" The boy stood up and said,

> Prayer is an offering up of our desires to God, for things agreeable to His will, in the name of Christ, with confessions of our sins and thankful acknowledgment to Him for His mercies.

The boy sat down and Moody was absolutely astonished that, without a moment's hesitation, he had recited the definition of prayer from the Shorter Catechism. He looked at the boy and said, "Be thankful, son, that you were born in Scotland"—a place where both prayer and the catechism were once taken very seriously.

---

1. John Piper, sermon manuscript on Colossians 4:2–4, www. desiringgod.org/ResourceLibrary/Sermons/ByScripture/2/2_ Devote_Yourselves_to_Prayer/

In his little book *Personal Declension and Revival of Religion in the Soul,* Octavius Winslow writes,

> True prayer is the aspiration of a renewed soul towards God; it is the breathing of Divine life, sometimes in the accents of sorrow, sometimes as the expressions of want, and always as the acknowledgment of dependence; it is the looking up of a renewed, afflicted, needy, and dependent child to its own loving heavenly Father, in all consciousness of utter weakness, and in all the sweetness of loving trust.[2]

Prayer is not incompatible with God's sovereignty, nor is prayer the means by which we selfishly obtain what we want from God. Rather, prayer is the means of grace by which a sovereign God gives us what He in His infinite wisdom deems best for us. Perhaps no place are these two truths more clearly taught than in John 15.

ANSWERED PRAYER AND COMMUNION WITH CHRIST

The key to answered prayer is abiding in Christ. That is the key to our motivation for prayer and the key to obtaining answers to prayer. In John 15:7, there's a precondition upon asking and receiving what we desire, and that precondition is abiding in Christ and having His Word abide in us. Abiding in Christ and seeking to fill our hearts with His Word results in the conforming of our thoughts and our affections, our attitudes and our actions, to Christ as Lord of all. It gives the Holy Spirit material to work with—material to apply the Word and will of God to our hearts and minds so

---

2. Octavius Winslow, *Personal Declension and Revival of Religion in the Soul* (Edinburgh: The Banner of Truth Trust, 1993), 91.

that we bear much fruit. This is the precondition for asking and receiving what we desire. The same idea occurs in Psalm 37:4: "Delight thyself also in the LORD, and he shall give thee the desires of thine heart."

Delighting in God results in the transformation of unholy desires into holy desires, desires that are consistent with the purposes of God. The thought in John 15:16 is similar: whatever you ask the Father in Christ's name He will give you.

Asking in the name of Christ is asking with an understanding and an appreciation of all that God is for us in Christ. It's asking consistently with all that our union with Christ implies, including the fact that Christ is the only Mediator between God and sinners. By Christ's obedience to God's holy law in the place of the sinner's disobedience and by His substitutionary death, He wins every right and privilege for sinners to be heard by God.

Every answer to prayer is bought and paid for by the blood of Christ, so any request which we offer that is inconsistent with the work and will of Christ, God will not answer. The motive of every request and every answer is the glory of God. God will not deny Himself or the work of His Son in order to answer prayers that are inconsistent with His will or to answer prayers that are wrongly motivated. In James 4:3, the Spirit says, "Ye ask, and receive not, because ye ask amiss [with wrong motives], that ye may consume it upon your lusts."

Are you spending your life for selfish pleasures, or are you spending your life for the pleasures of God? Are you living for the experience of vain pleasure that lasts only for a little while, or are you living to know and experience the glories of God and to make them known to others?

There's not a single prayer that God will answer when we're living for ourselves. Psalm 66:18 says, "If I regard [cherish] iniquity in my heart, the Lord will not hear me."

Cherishing God is the key to answered prayer. "And whatsoever ye shall ask in my name," Jesus says in John 14:13, "that will I do, that the Father may be glorified in the Son." Everything that the Son has done and continues to do is for the glory of the Father. So when we come to Christ in prayer, we must pray in a way that is consistent with all that God is for us and has done for us in His Son. Our satisfaction must be in Christ, in the One with whom God the Father is completely satisfied and has chosen to magnify. The basis of answered prayer is not our good works because even our best works are all tainted by imperfection; the basis of answered prayer is receiving in faith all that the Holy Spirit applies to us of the perfect work of God's own dear Son.

ANSWERED PRAYER AND COMMUNION
WITH THE HOLY SPIRIT

All sin is a violation of God's holy law, but Paul says that when we continue in sin, we grieve the person of the Holy Spirit. When we sin, we are not merely violating a principle or violating a holy standard; we are neglecting a person—we are wounding Him. "Grieve not the holy Spirit of God," Ephesians 4:30 says. "Quench not the Spirit," 1 Thessalonians 5:19 says.

Are you repenting of your sins of heart, mind, and tongue? Are you repenting of your secret sins, your lust and your covetousness, your pride and your self-reliance, your critical spirit and your critical words? Are you repenting of anger and impatience and discontentment? Are you repenting of the lack of poverty of spirit, the lack of meekness, the lack of mourning over sin, the lack of hungering and thirsting for righteousness, the lack of mercy, the lack of purity of heart, and an unwillingness to suffer for Christ's sake? Are you concerned at all that these and other sins are causing the Holy Spirit to withdraw from you?

In Psalm 51, David prays, "Cast me not away from thy presence; and take not thy holy spirit from me," and we imagine that his prayer cannot be for us as new covenant believers. But we fail to see what David is really praying. He's not describing being cast out of God's presence or having God remove His indwelling Holy Spirit, which would constitute a fall from grace and a loss of salvation. David is praying—as we should—that the Father would not remove the gracious effects of the Spirit's presence in our lives. John Stott once said that the "Holy Spirit is a sensitive Spirit. He hates sin, discord, and falsehood, and He shrinks away from them." Charles Hodge writes,

> The Holy Spirit's indwelling certifies that we are the children of God and secures our final salvation...to grieve Him, therefore, is to wound Him on whom our salvation depends. Though He will not finally withdraw from those in whom He dwells, yet when grieved, He withholds the manifestation of His presence.[3]

There's a great illustration of this in John Bunyan's book, *The Holy War*. His book is an allegory like *Pilgrim's Progress,* and it is written to awaken Christians from passivity and inactivity to diligence, zeal, and spiritual success. In it, Bunyan depicts the war between King Shaddai (God the

---

3. Arturo Arzudia, *Spirit Empowered Preaching: Involving the Holy Spirit in Your Ministry* (Ross-shire, Scotland: Christian Focus, 1998), 156.

Father) and Diabolus (Satan) for the soul of man. The soul of man is pictured as a town called Mansoul which lies between two worlds. The town of Mansoul was originally a beautiful castle but fell to Diabolus. Some time later, Prince Emmanuel (Christ) forces entry upon the city and several Diabolonians are killed, but Emmanuel remains encamped outside the city walls. The original inhabitants of Mansoul hold a conference and agree to petition the Prince for their lives. Emmanuel, along with Lord Secretary (the Holy Spirit), marches into Mansoul. Diabolus is made a prisoner and bound in chains. The inhabitants then request Emmanuel to take up residence among them. After Emmanuel and Lord Secretary enter, there is the struggle to put the remaining Diabolonians to death, and at one point Mr. Carnal-security prevails. Because of Carnal-security, the Prince is greatly offended and privately withdraws.

Diabolus increases his deception and the inhabitants of Mansoul grow weaker and weaker every day. One night, the inhabitants of Mansoul make a rash sortie against Diabolus and suffer great losses. Bunyan describes the condition of Mansoul as *winter* because Carnal-security has done so much damage. Finally, the inhabitants of Mansoul decide to petition Emmanuel once again. However, the first petition is sent, not because of an interest in the Prince, but only because of the trouble that Carnal-security has caused. So Prince Emmanuel pays no attention at all. They send another petition and it too is rejected. At one point, the road from Mansoul to the courts of King Shaddai is completely full of messengers going to and coming from the King, but none were permitted to enter the King's courts.

After being in such a sad and miserable condition for so long, the towns people call another meeting and agree to draw up one more petition. However, Mr. Godly-fear stands and says that he knows that his Lord, the Prince, never would receive a petition from anyone unless Lord Secretary's signature was on it. This, he said, was the reason why none of their other petitions had prevailed upon the Prince. Then they said that they would draw up another one and get Lord Secretary to sign it. But Mr. Godly-fear answers that Lord Secretary would not sign any petition that he had not had a part in composing and drawing up, and that the Prince knows Lord Secretary's signature from all the other signatures in the world and could not possibly be deceived by any pretense whatsoever. Therefore, his advice was to go to Lord Secretary and plead with him to lend them his aid.

Bunyan illustrates well the war that rages between the flesh and the spirit and our need for sincere and utter dependence upon the Spirit and the Word in order to grow in grace and communion with God. Only the prayer of faith prevails upon Christ. God hears our prayers when they pass from our hearts to the heart of Christ by means of the Spirit and the Word, and the heart from which the prayer of faith springs is not the heart that holds onto sin and self-will. The prayer of faith springs from a heart that puts the flesh and remaining sin to death, and the question we must ask ourselves is this: Am I engaged in this war for my soul through fervent faithful prayer?

Satan is a subtle, sleepless enemy of the soul, and he will do anything to get us to pray with wrong desires and wrong motives or to stop praying in private or never to start at all. John Livingstone once said that Satan either strikes at the root of faith, or at the root of diligence.[4]

---

4. David Macintyre, *The Hidden Life of Prayer* (Ross-shire,

Are your prayers motivated by a desire for communion with God, a desire to taste and see that the Lord is good? Do you get knots in your stomach at the thought of so wounding and grieving the Spirit of Christ that He withdraws from you? Then do not withhold prayer from God! Watch and pray that you do not fall into temptation. Wait upon God to work on your behalf. Pray with a sense of expectation and persevere in praying until God answers.

"PRAYING THROUGH"

Have you ever prayed and felt that your prayers didn't go past the ceiling? Older saints called praying until God answers with the felt presence of His Spirit "praying through."

One night several years ago, a young man awakened me in the wee hours of the morning with a sharp knock on my door. He was struggling intensely with temptation and wanted to talk. I invited him in and we talked. After about forty minutes, I felt that I had sufficiently answered his questions and I asked the young man if he'd like to pray. We prayed together for about twenty minutes and then I told him that we could talk more the next day. But the young man objected strongly, pleading with me, "Pastor, I don't feel that my prayers have gotten off the floor. God has not answered," he said. We began praying again and we prayed for another hour and a half. The time seemed to pass as if it were only a few moments because God broke through. He answered us! He met with us in the sweetness of felt communion. We each confessed our sins: our dullness of mind and heart, the chinks in our spiritual armor, and our not making use of Christ and the graces He gives for dealing

---

Scotland: Christian Focus, 1993), 52.

with our remaining sin, Satan, and the world. God broke through and ministered to us both. We each felt that we did not even need further sleep. The will of God in communing with Him in prayer was our food and drink and sleep. It was a glorious time of resolving in prayer to grow in holiness and to submit to one another in accountability for zero tolerance in areas of our common struggle with remaining sin.

More recently, another man in our church and I prayed for an hour one Friday and I never got a sense that God was answering me. We prayed again on Saturday morning and finally God answered. I confessed and grieved over my sins, and God granted tears of sorrow and joy and He granted cleansing and repentance. I prayed for revival and God refreshed me. We "prayed through" and enjoyed the felt presence of God's Spirit.

Isaiah 64:4 says that God works for those who wait for Him. It is God's way that we should persist in prayer, that we should persist in coming to Him and pleading with Him in order to enjoy His felt presence.

God certainly supports and sustains us in our weakness, but God also discerns the difference between the weakness of an immature faith and the wickedness of carnality in our lives. "God has mercy for the can-nots," says Samuel Bolton, "but none for the will-nots."[5]

When we give ourselves over to carnal security, it's then that our remaining sin and the uncrucified desires of our flesh get the upper hand in the war that rages against us. Inward heart conditions are far more dangerous to the well-being of our souls than we care to imagine. We may learn

---

5. Samuel Bolton, *The True Bounds of Christian Freedom* (Edinburgh: The Banner of Truth Trust, 1994), 43.

to avoid all public sin. However, it's not until we're moved away from superficial views of sin to a real view of sin and the sinful condition of our hearts that we begin to take the sins of our heart more seriously and consequently take the forgiving grace of God in the gospel more seriously. A real view of sin will inevitably turn us outside ourselves and selfish motives and turn us unto Christ. When armed with the truth, we recognize that the solution to all our sin is not in us, but in Christ and the gospel. We must not only give attention to the outward sins which others see, but to the inward sins of the heart, which is the source of all other sin.

When we neglect the sins of the heart and private prayer, which is our first defense, it is to the detriment of enjoying and communing with God. John Calvin once wrote,

> We lie on earth poor and famished, and almost destitute of spiritual blessings, while Christ now sits in glory at the right hand of the Father, and clothed with the highest majesty.... It ought to be imputed to our slothfulness and to the smallness of our faith.[6]

If we are spiritually poor, there can be no question who is to blame. We ourselves are to blame because we have not prayed as we ought.

It has been said that every sin problem is a prayer problem, and that there is no sin that we will ever commit that could not have been avoided by prayer. Think of it! Isn't that what Jesus taught in Matthew 6:13? "Lead us not into temptation, but deliver us from evil." Again, Calvin says that while we grow dull and stupid toward our miseries, God watches and keeps guard on our behalf, and sometimes even helps us unasked;

---

6. John Calvin, *Commentary on the Gospel According to John* (Grand Rapids: Baker Book House, 1998), 1:310.

and yet it is very important for us to call upon Him. Then he offers six reasons for persevering in prayer:

- First, that our hearts may be fired with a zealous and burning desire ever to seek, love, and serve Him, while we become accustomed in every need to flee to Him as a sacred anchor.

- Secondly, that there might not enter our hearts any desire and any wish at all of which we should be ashamed to make Him a witness, while we learn to set all our wishes before His eyes and even to pour out our whole hearts.

- Thirdly, that we prepare to receive His benefits with true gratitude of heart and thanksgiving, benefits that our prayer reminds us come from His hand.

- Fourthly, that, having attained what we were seeking and being convinced that He has answered our prayers, we should be led to meditate upon His kindness more ardently.

- Fifthly, that at the same time we embrace with greater delight those things which we acknowledge have been obtained by prayer.

- And finally, that use and experience may, according to the measure of our feebleness, confirm God's providence, while we understand not only that He promises never to fail us and of His own will opens the way to call upon Him at the very point of necessity, but also that He ever extends His hand to help His own, not wet-nursing them with words but defending them with present help.[7]

Prayer is the first expression of faith. It's the first evidence of spiritual life in our souls and the first step towards communion with God. So growth in prayer marks our

---

7. Calvin, *Institutes*, 3.20.3.

growth in grace and communion with God. It's inevitable: if we are not growing in prayer, growing in and enjoying both the spirit of prayer as well as the daily discipline of private prayer, then surely we are not growing in grace.

PRAYING WITH SPIRITUAL EYES

The year after I graduated seminary, I taught Physics and Bible in a small Christian school in Knoxville, Tennessee. That same year, we had a young man speak in chapel who had hiked all 2,160 miles of the Appalachian Trail as a south bounder. Not many people hike the southern route, especially alone, because of how late in the year you have to start. The pass in Northern Maine does not open early enough for hikers to get to the other end of the trail in North Georgia before it turns winter again. John, whose nickname was Trail-walker, was a converted Jewish man. He told us that he had prayed that God would grant him a burning bush experience like that of Moses, but disappointedly he thought that God had not met him in a burning bush. During John's talk, he said that God had used the one hundred days he spent in solitude to change his life forever. Think of it! He spent one hundred days on the trail—over three months—without seeing a single soul! Later, I told John that God had met him in the burning bush of solitude and prayer.

Do you spend time alone with God? What is it like? Does the God who is a river of delight and a fountain of life meet with you in the solitude of secret prayer? Are you enjoying communion with Him? Are you seeing Him in secret prayer with true spiritual eyes?

In college, I had a friend named George Harvey Bickley VI. We called him Dutch for short. We went to the same church together and the summer before we met, Dutch had an accident and nearly lost one of his eyes. While drilling a piece of metal, the drill shattered and part of it lodged in his right eye. A day or two after the operation to remove the metal, a pastor from a local church visited him and said something to him that was very instrumental in Dutch coming to Christ. Very boldly, the pastor told Dutch that perhaps God would allow his loss of sight physically in order to cause him to see through new spiritual eyes.

Perhaps the best biblical illustration of this is found in 2 Kings 6:8–20. The king of Syria was making war against Israel, and God revealed every movement of Syria's army to a prophet named Elisha. Elisha in turn would send warnings to the king of Israel. The king of Syria grew furious and thought that someone from within his own camp was betraying the movements of his army. However, his servants said to him that Elisha, the prophet of the God of Israel, knew the very words that the king of Syria was speaking in his own bedroom. So the king of Syria inquired as to where Elisha was; they told him the prophet was to be found in Dothan. Consequently, the king of Syria sent a great army, complete with horses and chariots, to capture Elisha and bring him back to Syria. That very night, the Syrian army surrounded the city of Dothan. Early the next morning, Elisha the man of God and his servant, Gehazi, arose and went out, and they saw that the city was surrounded by the army of Syria. Gehazi was fearful, but Elisha told him not to be afraid because those who were with them were greater than those who were against them. And Elisha prayed that the Lord would open his servant's eyes. The sovereign Lord did open Gehazi's eyes and he saw that the hills surrounding Elisha were full of horses and chariots of fire. Then Elisha prayed that the Lord would strike the Syrian soldiers with blindness. He walked right up to them and told them to follow him and he would lead them to the man for whom they were looking. Elisha led them right into the center of the city of Samaria. Then Elisha prayed again and their eyes were opened and they looked and saw that they were inside Samaria, standing before the king of Israel.

Elisha was a man of great faith, but whether great or small, God only works on our behalf when we seek Him in faith. You must spend time every day in communion with God, reading His Word, praying in the Spirit, and listening to His voice. Every day you must seek God in the solitude of private prayer. Let your prayers be characterized by reverence for God, humility, and brokenness because of the sinful condition of your heart. Plead with God that you might see His beauty and taste the glory of His sweet, free, sovereign grace. Beg God to draw near you in the sweetness of felt communion so that you might see His power and His glory and that He might satisfy you as David says in Psalm 63:5: with marrow and fatness so that you might praise Him with joyful lips. Jesus said in John 16.24, "Hitherto have ye asked nothing in my name: ask, and ye shall receive, that your joy may be full."

There is no secret to a life full of joy. It's simply to ask in faith and receive. Abide in Christ and allow His Word to abide in you, so that whenever you ask for what you desire, it will be done for you. Abide in Christ with reverent, patient, persevering, expectant prayer.

DISCUSS THE ISSUES

1. What is prayer? Why are prayer and the sovereignty of God not incompatible? If the key to answered prayer is abiding in Christ and letting His Word abide in us, what does that mean then?

2. How does cherished sin hinder prayer? How does unrepentant sin grieve the Holy Spirit? What is carnal security and how does it affect prayer? Why do prayers offered in persevering faith prevail upon Christ? How may we know when we are praying in faith or not? Put Calvin's six reasons for persevering in prayer in your own words.

3. What is the God-ward goal of prayer? What is the man-ward goal? What steps will you take to insure that you attain these two goals?

SOLVE THE SCENARIO

Ray is a young man in his early twenties who lives in a rural town in South Georgia named Wadley. Though he grew up going to church, he just recently became a Christian. From the moment they first met at work, Ray was drawn to Rev. Rev is an older man who has worked for thirty years at the saw-mill. He also pastors a fairly large country church in a rural community of mostly poor folks. Rev is very wise and very winsome; Ray has lunch with Rev as often as possible to talk to him about the Lord. One Friday evening late in the summer, the boss had a barbecue at his cabin and Ray was very glad to see that Rev was there. After dinner, the two of them walked down by the banks of the river to talk and pray. Ray had heard many people pray growing up in church, but he had never experienced anything like praying with Rev. When Rev prayed, his entire body trembled with awe in the presence of God, and he prayed with authority, power, and assurance as Ray had never known; when Rev spoke to God, he spoke to him as a man speaks with his closest friend. After they prayed together, Rev and Ray both became quiet and hardly spoke a word as they walked back to the boss's cabin. Ray treasured up the experience of praying which such a great man of God as Rev. On Monday at lunch, Ray told Rev that he'd never experienced the fullness of the presence of God as when they had prayed together. Ray confessed that he felt his own prayers to be more like a grocery list, asking God mostly for material things. Then Ray asked Rev to teach him to pray. Being as gracious a man as Rev is, he said, "It would be my great pleasure."

Try and put yourself in the place of Rev. What and how will you teach Ray?

SIT AT THE FEET OF CHRIST-CENTERED EXPERIENTIAL TEACHERS

The Hidden Life of Prayer, by D. M. McIntyre (*Level:* Basic)
  http://www.spiritone.com/~wing/hiddnint.htm

The Lord's Prayer: Its Spirit and Its Teaching, by Octavius Winslow (*Level:* Basic to Intermediate), www.gracegems.org/Winslows/lord_prayer.htm

Lord, Teach Us to Pray, by Alexander Whyte (*Level:* Basic to Intermediate) http://books.google.com/books?id=LD NU526deVsC&dq=%22lord+teach+us+to+pray%22+%22alexander+whyte%22&printsec=frontcover&source=web&ots=QMXIwaFxuj&sig=4gi7zkUL3UHIfhWBA1FcnrKUrEo#PPA3,M1

The Necessity of Prayer, by E. M. Bounds (*Level:* Basic),*www. leaderu.com/cyber/books/bounds/necessity.html*

Power through Prayer, by E. M. Bounds (*Level:* Basic), www. oldlandmarks.com/embpower.htm

What Happens When I Pray, by Thomas Goodwin and Benjamin Palmer (*Level:* Basic)

Valley of Vision: A Collection of Puritan Prayers and Devotions, by Arthur Bennett (*Level:* Basic to Intermediate)

Operation World: Twenty-first Century Edition, by Patrick Johnstone

A Method of Prayer, by Matthew Henry (*Level:* Basic to Intermediate)

A Theology of Prayer, by Benjamin Morgan Palmer (*Level:* Basic to Intermediate)

The Return of Prayers, by Thomas Goodwin (*Level:* Intermediate)

"Getting Started in Prayer," by Maurice Roberts (*Level:* Basic) http://www.banneroftruth.org/pages/articles/ article_detail.php?140

"A Call to Prayer," chapter 4 in *Practical Religion,* by J. C. Ryle (*Level:* Basic) www.gracegems.org/SERMONS/ call_to_prayer.htm

"The Preciousness of Prayer," chapter 10 in *The Precious Things of God,* by Octavius Winslow (*Level:* Basic to Intermediate) http://www.gracegems.org/W/p10.htm

A Hunger for God: Desiring God through Fasting and Prayer, by John Piper (*Level:* Basic to Intermediate)

The Lord's Prayer, by Thomas Watson (*Level:* Basic to Intermediate)

"Prayer: Fasting and Meditation," a set of messages on mp3 by John Piper http://www.biblicaltraining. org/audio/TH520/Prayer_1a001.mp3 http://www. biblicaltraining.org/audio/TH520/Prayer_1b001.

mp3 http://www.biblicaltraining.org/audio/TH520/
Prayer_2001.mp3 http://www.biblicaltraining.
org/audio/TH520/Prayer_3001.mp3 http://www.
biblicaltraining.org/audio/TH520/Prayer_4001.mp3

"Prayer," mp3 message by Dr. Martyn Lloyd Jones http://
berbc.org/onlinesermons/Dr%20Martyn%20Lloyd%2
0Jones/LJ03_PrayerFor.mp3

"The Word of God and Family Prayer," by Thomas
Doolittle (*Level:* Basic to Intermediate) http://www.
mountzion.org/fgb/Summer04/FgbS6-04.html

"Motives for Family Worship," in *Family Worship*, by Dr.
J. Merle D'Aubigne, (*Level:* Basic to Intermediate)
http://www.apuritansmind.com/TheChristianFamily/
DAubigneMerleMotivesFamilyPrayer.htm

The Privy Key to Heaven, by Thomas Brooks (*Level:* Basic
to Intermediate) http://www.gracegems.org/Brooks/
privy_key_of_heaven.htm

Matthew 26:41

Watch and pray, that ye enter not into temptation: the spirit indeed is willing, but the flesh is weak.

1 Peter 4:7

Be ye therefore sober, and watch unto prayer.

1 Thessalonians 5:16–18

Rejoice evermore. [17]Pray without ceasing. [18]In every thing give thanks: for this is the will of God in Christ Jesus concerning you.

CHAPTER ELEVEN

A Guide for Personal Daily Prayer

GUIDE THREE

THIS SIMPLE PLAN follows the ACTS acrostic—Adoration, Confession, Thanksgiving, and Supplication (or Petition). In private prayer as well as public prayer, the first words from our lips should be a request that the Holy Spirit incline our hearts to God and open our understanding that we might apprehend His greatness and our need for Him. Prayer for the Christian ought always to be framed and saturated with Scripture, so I've provided a few Scripture references which correspond to each matter in prayer. I want to encourage you in your personal study to add to the list of Scripture references and even to add to the outline. Pray through Scripture. You may easily take a passage of Scripture and turn every statement in it into a cause for adoration and praise, confession, thanksgiving, and petition. If we use as much Scripture as possible in prayer, it will move us away from our inherent man-centeredness and our tendency to treat prayer as a grocery list of requests, and it will move us toward a thoroughly biblical, God-centered life of prayer.

I. ADORATION

- Begin by asking God to incline your heart to worship Him, to enjoy the sweet communion of His presence, to behold His wonders, and marvel at Him (Josh. 24:23; 1 Kings 8:57–58; Ps. 88:2, 119:36, 119:18, 86:11, 90:14; Eph. 1:8; 3:16; John 15:7).

- Then reverently, in humble adoration, acknowledge God's existence (Heb. 11:6).

- Praise Him for His greatness, confessing that we may know Him personally, but that His judgments and His ways are beyond our ability as His creatures to know fully or comprehensively (1 Chron. 29:10–14; Job 11:7; Ps. 145:3; Isa. 55:8–9).

- Praise each of His attributes (Ps. 29, 96): spirituality (John 4:24); knowledge (Ps. 147:5); wisdom (Rom. 11:33–36); veracity (John 17:17); goodness (Matt. 5:44–45); common grace (Acts 14:17); love (Rom. 5:8; 2 Cor. 5:14–15); special grace (Eph. 2:5–9); mercy (Rom. 11:30–32); longsuffering (2 Pet. 3:9); majestic holiness (Isa. 6:1–7); ethical holiness (Hab. 1:13); absolute righteousness (Ps. 145:17); relative righteousness (Rom. 2:6); will (Eph. 1:11–12); power (Luke. 1:37); self-existence (John 5:26); immutability (James 1:17); infinity (Matt. 5:48); unity (1 Cor. 8:6).

- Acknowledge Him as Creator and Sustainer of life, and praise Him for His providential care, both His sweet as well as His dark providences (Ps. 8, 19; Rom. 8:28–32).

- Confess His authority, His right, and His power to rule over you (Matt. 10:28, 28:18–20).

- Praise God as the fountain of spiritual life and as a river of delight (Ps. 16:11, 36:8–9).

- Give honor to each member of the Trinity and to their separate works (2 Cor. 13:14; Eph. 1:3–23; 1 John 5:7).

- Acknowledge your total dependence upon Him; God is glorified in our dependence upon Him (Ps. 100:3; Isa. 43:7; Acts 17:28).

II. CONFESSION

- Confess your acts of sin and the sinfulness of your condition and acknowledge both as reprehensible to the holiness of God and deserving of His wrath and punishment (Ps. 32, 51, 130:3; Gal. 5:19–21; Col. 3:5–11; Rom. 7:24).

- Confess the shame and guilt of sin (Rom. 6:21, 7:7–13) and the lack of humility before God (Rom. 3:19); sorrow for sin (2 Cor. 7:10); hatred of sin (Ezek. 36:31).

- Confess secret sin, cherishing sin, covering sin, and justifying sin (Ps. 66:18; James 2:10).

- Confess selfishness, covetousness, anger, envy, pride, lust... (James 1:20; 4:6–10).

- Confess spiritual dullness, apathy, passivity, complacency, spiritual drought, coldness, indifference, hardness of heart, and lack of spiritual discipline (1 Cor. 3:1–3; Heb. 2:1–4, 5:12–14).

- Confess worldliness (James 4:4), sensuality (James 5:5), flesh-pleasing (Rom. 8:5).

- Confess the lack of desire for God's Word, to read it, to understand it, to meditate on it, and to memorize it (Josh. 1:8; Amos 8:11; Ps. 1; 2 Tim. 2:15).

- Confess sins that hinder private, family, and corporate worship, and sins of lack of preparation for worship (Judg. 10:13; 1 Sam. 7:3; Ezra 7:10; Job 11:13–14; Jer. 2:13; John 8:19).

- Confess sins that hinder others (Matt. 7:1–5; Rom. 14:13; 1 Cor. 8:13).

- Confess lack of faith, smallness of faith, worry, and anxiety (Isa. 26:3; Matt. 6:28–34).

- Acknowledge the need of the Spirit of God to search your life through and through, then confess sins of ignorance and omission (Ps. 139).

- Confess pardon because of the blood and righteousness of Christ (Rom. 3–5).

III. THANKSGIVING

- Thank God for His benefits in general (Ps. 103:1–2).

- Give thanks to God for the nearness of His presence (Num. 6:23–27; Ps. 75:1).

- Thank God for designing salvation, providing His own Son as our Redeemer, and applying the work of redemption to you by His Spirit (Eph. 1:3–14).

- Offer thanks for the person and work of Christ, and in particular for Christ fully satisfying all God's just demands for your salvation (Rom. 5:8).

- Thank God for His covenant grace and covenant love by which He forgives and draws near us as sinners (Ps. 36; Eph. 2:11–13).

- Thank Him for sending His Spirit and for His ongoing work (John 16:13–15).

IV. SUPPLICATION

- Plead with God for the work of the Spirit in making the surpassing riches of Christ known, longed for, hoped in, and treasured much (John 16:13–15).

- Pray for the enjoyment of communion with God (John 15:7; 2 Cor. 13:12).

- Beg God for spiritual apprehension, spiritual power, and spiritual thirst, and ask Him to deliver you from the spiritually deadening effects of moralism and naturalism, and the corrupting influences of sin, the flesh, the world, and Satan (1 Cor. 2:9–16; 1 Cor. 2:4–5; Rom. 15:13; Matt. 5:6).

- Press God to help you to know yourself as loved because of His covenant love (Eph. 2:4–9; 2 Cor. 5:14–15).

- Petition God for the apprehension of the greatness of the gospel, the relation of justification to sanctification, and that all Christians might live holy lives with proper motives and motivation (2 Cor. 5:14–15).

- Pray for the faithful proclamation of the law and the gospel, the establishing of Christ's church, and the expansion of the church (Matt. 28:18–20).

- Pray that the Word of God might run and have success (Col. 4:2–6).

- Intercede for those who will be counted worthy to suffer martyrdom (Rev. 6:11).

- Pray for your immediate family, extended family, neighbors, and each member of your church family (2 John 2; Philemon 25).

- Pray for spiritual leaders and complementary roles in the family (Eph. 5:22–6:4).

- Pray for the church to be established in grace, love, and unity (1 Tim. 3:14–15).

- Pray for pastors and missionaries (Rom. 15:30–33).

- Pray for the revival of true religion among God's people and the salvation of the lost (Ps. 80, 143:11; 1 Pet. 4:17; Luke 19:10).

- Pray for world leaders and leaders of our country, state, and city (1 Tim. 2:1–2).

- Close with a desire for God's blessing (Num. 6:23– 27; Jude 24–25; Heb. 13:20–21).

Psalm 1

Blessed is the man that walketh not in the counsel of the ungodly, nor standeth in the way of sinners, nor sitteth in the seat of the scornful. ²But his delight is in the law of the LORD; and in his law doth he meditate day and night. ³And he shall be like a tree planted by the rivers of water, that bringeth forth his fruit in his season; his leaf also shall not wither; and whatsoever he doeth shall prosper. ⁴The ungodly are not so: but are like the chaff which the wind driveth away. ⁵Therefore the ungodly shall not stand in the judgment, nor sinners in the congregation of the righteous. ⁶For the LORD knoweth the way of the righteous: but the way of the ungodly shall perish.

CHAPTER TWELVE

The Grace of Law

OR, THE BLESSEDNESS OF
DELIGHTING IN GOD'S LAW

MY WIFE, PAULA, and I have friends who live in the hills of North Carolina whose names are Kirk and Konnie. They own a campground nestled up in those hills. Several years ago, they invited our family to spend a Thursday night with them and go snow-skiing the next day. Early Friday morning, all the guys piled into Kirk's car and all the girls piled into our car and we started the drive up. On the way out of their drive, Kirk said, "Murray, I want to show you something. See that little hut right there?" It was a tiny, one-room hut made of block with a tin roof, about three hundred yards away from Kirk and Konnie's home. He said, "The man who lives there is seventy years old and he's lived there for forty years with no electricity and no running water. His name is Ab, and over the last three years we've sought to befriend him. We ran water over to his little house and offered to run electricity, but you know, he wouldn't take it. He has a little moped and once every other week or so, he goes to town to buy milk and a few other things. One day, Konnie asked him how he kept his milk from going bad without a refrigerator." Ab said, "Well, missy, I just learned to drink it sour."

The spiritual lives of a lot of people are just like that. They have settled for a "sour Christ" in the place of a "sweet Christ." They've also settled for a sour life instead of a life sweetened by the blessedness of delighting in God and in His law.

Psalm 1 stands like a sentinel for the rest of the Psalms, and it confronts everyone who enters and seeks to identify with God's people with two fundamental choices: to taste sweetness in God's law which alone gives meaning and purpose in this life and in the life to come; or turn in disobedience away from God's law, live a fruitless life, then stare ultimate judgment and hell square in the face. In this chapter, I want us to look at the grace of delight, or the blessedness of delighting in God's law.

THE WAY OF LIFE FOR THE GODLY CONSIDERED NEGATIVELY

The godly person does not walk in the counsel of the wicked, he does not stand in the path of sinners, and he does not sit in the seat of scoffers. Derek Kidner comments that the words *counsel, way,* and *seat* draw our attention to our way of thinking, our way of behaving, and our way of belonging. These three indicate where our fundamental allegiance lies.[1] They indicate the direction that our heads and our hearts and our wills are going.

The godly person recognizes also that he or she is a sinner saved by grace. There is no personal goodness in him that would cause him to look down on others. He understands that he is a blood-washed sinner. For that reason, he cannot

---

1. Derek Kidner, *Psalms 1–72: An Introduction and Commentary* (Downers Grove, IL: Inter-Varsity Press, 1973), 47.

totally separate himself from unsaved people. However, he understands that, in order to live a godly life, he must practice some degree of separation from them.[2] So he does not walk in their counsel or highly regard those who disregard God and His Word. Neither does he stand in their path. He does not hang around the wrong crowd. Finally, he does not make the most fatal mistake of adopting the wrong crowd as those to whom he belongs.[3]

Here David shows a progression of sliding down the slippery slope of ungodliness by telling us what a godly person avoids. He does not avoid all contact with sinners, but he avoids listening to their counsel, being a party to their ways, adopting their attitude towards God and His law, or finding significance and security in their company.

Now, not only does David reveal the progression towards ungodliness, he also shows degrees of ungodliness, and we will find this progression helpful in learning to avoid ungodliness in all its degrees. The first word, *ungodly,* stands for all that is opposite God's character. The second word, *sinner,* indicates an even stronger opposition to God and His law. It often refers to utter lawlessness. Then finally, *scornful* is the most scandalous of all ungodly people. He is the farthest from God, the farthest from obedience to God's law, the farthest from repentance. He actively mocks God and seeks to lead others away from God. So the godly man or woman or boy or girl is known by avoiding the slippery slope of ungodliness and the kinds of relationships with sinners that would lead them away from God.

Perhaps we can all claim negative purity.[4] However,

---

2. Spurgeon, *Treasury of David,* 1:2.
3. Kidner, *Psalms 1–72,* 48.
4. Spurgeon, *Treasury of David,* 1:2.

avoiding what is wrong is only half the equation for godliness, and many wrongly build their hopes of heaven upon this cracked foundation. You can die just as easily from not eating good food as you can from drinking poison.[5] By merely avoiding evil, you may still go straight to hell. Therefore, may we never build our lives on the quicksand of merely avoiding the great negatives of sacred Scripture—the great "thou shalt nots." May our spiritual life not consist merely in what we are not doing. May there always be the right balance between avoiding what is wrong and seeking with all our heart what is right and good in the sight of God. May we see that the other half of the equation is equally necessary: that our supreme delight must be in the law of God!

THE WAY OF LIFE FOR THE
GODLY CONSIDERED POSITIVELY

The Psalmist writes in verse 2, "But his delight is in the law of the LORD, and in his law doth he meditate day and night." How are we to understand delighting in God's law? There are so many things we delight in, but delight in God's law exceeds them all. Psalm 19:10 says that the law of God is "more to be desired than gold, yea, than much fine gold: sweeter also than honey and the honeycomb."

It would be easy to understand if the psalmist was saying this of the grace of God, or of the love of God, or of the presence of God; but he is describing God's moral law.[6] We can understand that a person might respect God's

---

5. Thomas Watson, *The Saint's Spiritual Delight and A Christian on the Mount* (London, England: The Religious Tract Society, 1830), 8.
6.C. S. Lewis, *Reflections on the Psalms* (New York: A Harvest Book, 1986), 55.

moral law and seek to keep it, but it's hard to understand how we might find God's law more desirable than gold and more delicious than honey. How can the pleasure of God's law and obedience to it be stronger than the desire for food or stronger than the desire to be with a person whom you love? In *Reflections on the Psalms*, C. S. Lewis illustrates the difficulty like this. Lewis says,

> Think of a man held back by his unfortunate marriage to a crazy person or a criminal from a woman whom he may faithfully love. Or consider a hungry man left alone, without money, in a bakery with all that smell of fresh baked pastries wafting him in the face, and fresh bread, fresh cream and fresh strawberries sitting on the counter. How can these find the command against adultery or theft anything at all like honey? They may respect God's law, they may even obey it dutifully...but how can they find it enjoyable and sweet?[7]

Some would describe delight in the law of God as the satisfaction of a clean conscience for having obeyed. William Wordsworth calls this the "smile on duty's face, the smile that comes across our faces when we carry out our duty."[8] But that's not at all what the psalmist is saying here. Surely duty is implied; however, it's not first of all the duty, but God's law itself, in which he delights.

We have a number of musicians in our church, and some liken the way the psalmist feels about the law of God to the delight a musician takes in rehearsing a piece of music over and over before performing it flawlessly at a recital or before a crowd. The pleasure there is two-fold: the pleasure which

---

7. Ibid., 55; some wording changed for clarity.
8. Ibid., 56; Lewis is quoting William Wordsworth.

comes from getting it right and the pleasure which comes from the applause of others. However, the psalmist's delight is not said to be the delight of perfecting obedience, and certainly not the pleasure which comes from the approval of others for having performed well. The language that he uses in Psalms 1, 19, and 119 is the language of a person who is ravished by the moral beauty of God's law and the order and beauty that it brings to his own life as he conforms his heart, mind, and will to it. Delighting in God's law is experiencing personally the moral excellence of His law. It's recognizing that no one can improve on it. It is comprehending the greatness of God's law in contrast to the laws of man and man-centered religion, the difference being greater by far than cold clear water from a mountain spring to the stagnant stinking water of a sewer pond.

The word *delight* expresses the experience of taking emotional pleasure or emotional satisfaction in the law of God. In his little book, *The Life of God in the Soul of Man,* Henry Scougal says, "The worth and excellency of a soul is to be measured by the object of its love,"[9] and "the most ravishing pleasures, the most solid and substantial delights of which a human being is capable, are those which arise from the endearments of a well-placed and successful affection."[10]

God has placed the affection of delight in every human being, but by nature we delight in everything but God and His law. However, through the experience of the new birth, God rewrites His law upon our hearts and places a new and holy affection within the core of our being which delights in the law of God as the rule of life for the believer. In Jeremiah

---

9. Henry Scougal, *The Life of God in the Soul of Man* (Harrisonburg, VA: Sprinkle Publications, 1986), 66.
10. Ibid.

31:33, God says that He will put his law in our inward parts, and write it in our hearts; and He will be our God, and we shall be His people. The Apostle Paul echoes this same idea in Romans 7. Although he struggles to keep God's law as he should, he writes in verse 22, "I delight in the law of God after the inward man."

The great Puritan Thomas Watson preached a sermon on Psalm 1 called "The Saint's Spiritual Delight." In it he said,

> A child of God, though he cannot serve the Lord perfectly, yet he serves Him willingly; his will is in the law of the Lord; he is not a pressed soldier, but a volunteer, and by the beating of this kind of pulse, we may judge whether there is spiritual life in us or not. And if we have spiritual life in us, we will not only see obedience to God's law as our duty, but as our recreation.[11]

Horatius Bonar echoes this same thought in his little book *God's Way of Holiness*. "A forgiven man is the true worker," he says, "the true law-keeper. He can, he will, he must work for God. He has come into contact with the part of God's character which warms his cold heart."[12]

It's utterly impossible to judge true godliness by what we will to do with only lukewarm interest or with dogged dutiful obedience. John Murray keenly observes this fundamental truth in an introductory chapter in his book on Christian ethics.

> There is no conflict between the gratification of desire and the enhancement of his pleasure, on the one hand, and the fulfillment of God's command on the other.

---

11. Watson, *The Saint's Spiritual Delight*, 3.
12. Horatius Bonar, *God's Way of Holiness* (Ross-shire, Great Britain: Christian Focus, 1999), 58–59

Rather, the consciousness of compliance with divine command fortified and confirmed him the propriety and piety of the pleasure enjoyed. It is a strange deflection of thought that leads students of biblical ethics to set up an antithesis between impulse arising from sense of duty and the impulse of love and delight. The tension that often exists within us between a sense of duty and wholehearted spontaneity is a tension that arises from sin and a disobedient will. No such tension would have invaded the heart of un-fallen man. And the operations of saving grace are directed to the end of removing that tension so that there may be, as there was with man at the beginning, the perfect complementation of duty and pleasure, of commandment and love.[13]

Do you know this perfect complement between duty and delight? Has the boundless generosity of God warmed your cold heart so that you have become a true law-keeper? Is God's moral law your recreation? What a strange idea this is, especially to us Americans who live in a country where we have whatever else our heart could desire for recreation at our fingertips. But the psalmist insists that the law of God drowns all other delights!

In Isaiah 7:13, the Holy Spirit says that, without this holy delight, we weary ourselves and we weary God. Thomas Watson illustrated it like this. "If you had a friend who said, 'Come and visit me and I will supply you with all the money you want to do whatever your heart desires,' would you not go and visit, and would you not do whatever you could to show your gratitude? In God we have One who has supplied us with treasures far greater than any amount of money could

---

13. John Murray, *Principles of Conduct: Aspects of Biblical Ethics* (Grand Rapids: Eerdmans, 1991), 38–39.

ever buy."[14] In His moral law, He shows us what He's really like. He's infinitely holy in all His ways, so morally good that He cannot even look upon sin (Hab. 1:13), so morally pure that He dwells in unapproachable light (1 Tim. 6:16). He's also majestically holy, so high and exalted above His creation that heaven is His throne and earth His footstool (Isa. 66:1). So imposing is His majesty that the train of His kingly robe fills all the available space in the temple (Isa. 6:1). Yet this great God grants sinners like us the privilege of drawing near Him and enjoying Him through the grace of God in law and gospel. So Watson adds, "When we delight in God's moral law, that God twists His glory and our good together."[15]

We often look at obedience to the law of God in the wrong way. We view our obedience to the moral law as mere duty rather than the means of grace God intended for us to use to find our greatest pleasure and treasure in Him. As a prime example, compare your view of the Lord's Day with God's view. In Isaiah 58:13, the Spirit of God takes the fourth commandment and twists God's glory and our good together. He says,

> If thou turn away thy foot from the sabbath, from do-
> ing thy pleasure on my holy day; and call the sabbath
> a delight, the holy of the LORD, honourable; and shalt
> honour him, not doing thine own ways, nor finding
> thine own pleasure, nor speaking thine own words:
> [14]then shalt thou delight thyself in the LORD; and I will
> cause thee to ride upon the high places of the earth,

14. Watson, *The Saint's Spiritual Delight,* 10.
15. Ibid, 26.

and feed thee with the heritage of Jacob thy father: for the mouth of the LORD hath spoken it.

To take delight in God's law means that we take "exquisite pleasure" in it, and Isaiah reasons that when we take exquisite pleasure in God's law, we take exquisite pleasure in God Himself.

To delight in God's law means that we are overwhelmed by a sense of beauty and glory in God and in His works. I remember being overwhelmed when Sinclair Ferguson once said in a sermon, "We honor evangelical saints of days gone by who loved the worship of God on the Lord's Day, but we find practically incomprehensible their desire to squeeze every last moment out of congregational foretastes of eternal glory. Have you ever in the dying embers of Sunday night, rested your head on your pillow with wet eyes because the day of congregating in the presence of God does not last forever? Are we in danger of being so squeezed into the world's mold that Christ has this against us: we have lost our first love? Or do we still believe here and now that in God's presence is fullness of joy and at His right hand there are pleasures forevermore?"

Each of the Ten Commandments and whatever else God commands in His moral law may be applied in this same way: as a means of grace by which we become overwhelmed with a sense of beauty and glory in God. Use the law as God intended. Discover how God twists His glory and your good together in each of His commands. And do not settle for a sour life because you have settled for a sour view of the glory of God revealed in His law, but sweeten your life daily by the blessedness of delighting in God and in His law.

DISCUSS THE ISSUES

1. With what two fundamental choices does Psalm 1 confront us? Why is negative purity a cracked foundation upon which to build our hope of heaven? Why is negative purity not enough to make us holy?

2. What does the moral law of God represent? How does grace restore pleasure in God's law? How does the law become a necessary instrument of grace? Describe the experience of delighting in God's law. Why must we take exquisite pleasure in the law of God in order to take exquisite pleasure in God?

3. Read Luke 9:23–24 and 2 Corinthians 5:14–15 and explain how God twists His glory and our good together in the command to deny ourselves.

SOLVE THE SCENARIO

Gary and Ray became roommates two summers ago. They get along fairly well, but often get into animated—sometimes even heated—discussions about the role of law in the life of the believer. Gary believes that all the laws of the Old Testament, moral and civil, ought to be kept. The only exceptions for New Testament believers are the ceremonial laws which Gary regards to have been fulfilled by Christ. Ray doesn't believe any Old Testament laws are for New Testament believers, but that believers now live under a higher law which he regards to be the law of love. Ray tells Gary that he takes the Bible too literal at times and tries his best to show him that he ought to take the literal parts literally and the figurative parts figuratively. Gary chides Ray for being antinomian (against law) and Ray chides Gary for being legalistic. A third roommate, Ben, joined these two in their apartment. The guys recently asked Ben to lead a Bible study on Monday nights and you guessed it, the topic they chose for Ben is "the role of law in the life of the believer."

Cast yourself in the role of Ben and help Gary and Ray sort out what laws have passed away, what laws believers are bound to keep, the relationship between law and gospel, and what it means to offer God gospel obedience.

SIT AT THE FEET OF CHRIST-CENTERED EXPERIENTIAL TEACHERS

"The Saint's Spiritual Delight," a sermon on Psalm 1 by Thomas Watson (*Level:* Basic to Intermediate), www.biblebb.com/files/TW/tw-spiritual-delight.htm

"The Saint and the Law," chapter 5 in *God's Way of Holiness,* by Horatius Bonar (*Level:* Basic to Intermediate)

"Civic Law, Ceremonial and Moral," chapter 1 in *No Holiness, No Heaven,* by Richard Alderson (*Level:* Basic), www.the-highway.com/law1_Alderson.html

"The Moral Law a Rule of Obedience," chapter 2 in *The True Bounds of Christian Freedom,* by Samuel Bolton, (*Level:* Intermediate), www.the-highway.com/articleFeb00.html

The True Bounds of Christian Freedom, by Samuel Bolton, (*Level:* Intermediate)

"Introductory Essay" and chapter 8 entitled "Law and Grace" in *Principles of Conduct,* by John Murray (*Level:* Basic to Intermediate)

Volume III, book IV, chapter 1, entitled, "The Nature of Sanctification and Gospel Holiness Explained," book IV, chapter 2, entitled, "Sanctification, A Progressive Work," in *The Holy Spirit, vol. 3,* by John Owen, *The Works of John Owen* (*Level:* Intermediate to Difficult)

The Gospel Mystery of Sanctification, by Walter Marshall [This entire book ought to be read and reread, and especially Directions IX–XII on the comforts of the gospel and the duties of the law. The great Scottish theologian John Murray was once asked to give his recommendation on the best book on sanctification outside Scripture, and he said without hesitation it is this book by Marshall.] (*Level:* Intermediate to Difficult)

"Law Death, Gospel Life: Or, The Death of Legal Righteousness, The Life of Gospel Holiness," sermon in volume 2 of *The Works of Ralph Erskine* (*Level:* Intermediate)

"The Law and the Gospel," by John Colquhoun (*Level:* Intermediate), www.the-highway.com/lawandgospel_ Colquhoun.html

"Evangelical Obedience," chapter 10 in *Practical Christianity,* by A. W. Pink (*Level:* Basic to Intermediate)

"The Law and the Law of Love," chapter 1 in *True Spirituality,* by Francis Schaeffer [In it Schaeffer explains the relationship between law and love as it relates especially to the tenth commandment which he calls "the hub of the wheel." He then offers two tests for true spirituality: first, "Do I love God enough to be content?" and secondly, "Do I love others enough not to envy?"] (*Level:* Intermediate)

"Our Lord's Understanding of the Law of God," chapter 7 in *Honoring the Written Word of God,* by J. I. Packer (*Level:* Intermediate)

"Of Gospel Holiness; Implanted in the Heart, and Continued in the Whole Walk of Life," by Thomas Goodwin in *The Works of Thomas Goodwin;* 7:131–336, (*Level:* Intermediate to Difficult)

"The Marrow Controversy," three mp3 messages by Sinclair Ferguson's www.sermonaudio.com or www.mountzion. org

Job 22:21–26

Acquaint now thyself with him, and be at peace: thereby good shall come unto thee. ²²Receive, I pray thee, the law from his mouth, and lay up his words in thine heart. ²³If thou return to the Almighty, thou shalt be built up, thou shalt put away iniquity far from thy tabernacles. ²⁴Then shalt thou lay up gold as dust, and the gold of Ophir as the stones of the brooks. ²⁵Yea, the Almighty shall be thy defence, and thou shalt have plenty of silver. ²⁶For then thou shalt have thy delight in the Almighty, and shalt lift up thy face unto God.

CHAPTER THIRTEEN

Lay Your Gold in the Dust, Then God Himself will be Your Finest Gold

FINAL MEDITATION

IN THE BOOK OF JOB, Eliphaz and his friends argue with Job, taking the moral high ground and criticizing him without mercy. There's very little wrong with what they say, although they misapply much of their counsel in Job's situation. Unlike Job, their lives have been nothing but smooth sailing. With hardly any knowledge of their own inner corruption and very little experience of the chastening love of God, they sit in judgment of Job who was under severe trial and would soon be aware of more hidden faults than he ever imagined. At the beginning of chapter 22, Eliphaz is very hard on Job, but when you get to the end of the chapter, you can almost forgive all his harsh, unjust, critical words, because he finds such a degree of happiness in God as can hardly be imagined by Job or anyone. Charles Spurgeon called it a pasture of pleasure on the hilltops.[1]

---

1. Charles Haddon Spurgeon, *The Metropolitan Tabernacle Pulpit* (Pasadena: Pilgrim Publications, 1986), 31:332.

THE COMMAND TO KNOW AND LOVE GOD

Job 22:21–26 is counsel from a friend at its finest. If you would seek to counsel a friend in trouble, you would do well to paint a picture of the misery of sin as Job's friend does. You would do well to proclaim the terrors of God's holy law and the just condemnation he or she will surely incur if they should fail to repent. But if you would seek to lead your friend to true repentance, dare not leave off infinite pleasure offered in a relationship with God. Taking pleasure in God is our chief motive for repentance, faith, and fellowship with Him!

This friend's best counsel begins with the command to know and love God. The same word for *know* is used in Psalm 139:3 where God knows the psalmist's ways. Twice it's used for knowing intimately and therefore cherishing. So here's a command to know God *experientially* and *intimately* and to seek to be at peace with Him. In other words, get to know God; set your affections on Him and stop acting in opposition to Him. Cease your unholy war against God. Only then will the greatest possible good come to you.

This is not only the counsel of encouragement at its finest; it's also Hebrew poetry at its finest. As it often does, the second line in Hebrew poetry repeats the first and leaves no doubt in the readers' minds as to the author's true meaning. Do you desire to receive your greatest good from God? Then as the good poet adds in verse 22, receive instruction from the mouth of God and treasure up His words in your heart. When we take pleasure in His kingship and submit to His rule, then He keeps us in His love.

THE COMMAND TO REPENT
OF YOUR EARTHLY TREASURES

If you find a friend out of fellowship with God and your

counsel to him does not include an encouragement to repent, then your counsel would be lacking. Job's friends' counsel includes the command to repent, not merely of outward sinful actions, but also of earthly treasures. And notice that the command is not merely to turn from sin and sinful desires but to turn towards God. "Return to the Almighty," he says. Our repentance is always incomplete if we merely turn from sin and do not turn to the Lord. And this poet describes repentance in two ways. First, repentance is removing unrighteousness far from your life, far from the place in which you live, far from the sphere of family influence and from the influence of your church family. Secondly, repentance is laying your greatest treasures in the dust. Anything which takes the rightful place of God in your heart has to be laid down.

Job's friend is right. We lose our moral high ground when we hold any earthly treasure too tightly. We forfeit our moral and spiritual authority when we live in unholiness. And there's always the devil to pay, because we forfeit our freedom for bondage and fear—fear that we'll lose our unholy pleasures and unholy treasures, fear that what brings us ungodly security, significance, and satisfaction will be taken from us.

On January 8, 1956, when Jim Elliot was killed by the Auca Indians, what was most important to him was not taken from him. It was he who wrote, "He is no fool to give what he cannot keep; to gain what he cannot lose." A pastor friend recently said to his congregation that anything in their lives that they're unwilling to give up or give away for the sake of Christ and the progress of the gospel has too great a hold on them. Is there anything in your life that is more important to you than being in a right relationship with

God? Are earthly treasures and pleasures taking the place of God? Then you must lay them in the dust.

THE PROMISE THAT GOD WILL BE YOUR FINEST TREASURE

Job 22:25–26 contains the greatest motive to lay our gold in the dust and the greatest encouragement to live in constant communion with God. It's the promise that God will be our greatest treasure. The Spirit of God says that the Almighty will be our gold and our precious silver, and then we will have our delight in Him. It is so easy for us to hold on too tightly to temporary earthly treasures and sin by cherishing them excessively. But when we put away the sin of cherishing earthly treasures, then God and the rich abundance of all that He is will be our imperishable treasure and our greater and everlasting delight.[2]

Is God your greatest gold? Is He your all-in-all? It's so easy to prop ourselves up with anything that will make us outwardly happy. But what happens when the things that make you outwardly happy are taken away? Do you rest in the goodness of God? Can you say that the Lord is your best portion? Do you delight in the Almighty?

When we take delight in God, we're not simply glad that there is a God; we're glad that God is *our* God and we receive Him as He really is—*the Sovereign Lord!* We come to know and depend upon the God of the Bible and not our own imagination and we learn to savor Him as our Sovereign, not simply as our Savior. Charles Spurgeon once said, "It is as easy to make an idol out of your own thought as it is for

---

2. Franz Delitzsch, *Biblical Commentary on the Book of Job* (Whitefish, MT: Kessinger Publishing Co., 2006), 1:444.

the Hindu to make a god of mud out of the Ganges. There is but one God revealed in Holy Scripture, in Nature and in Providence. His name is Jehovah!"[3] When we delight in God, we treasure all His attributes equally. We take pleasure supremely in God, but we also take pleasure in all His works of creation and providence. We do not question His designs or rail against Him when we are under His fatherly discipline, for He chastens those whom He loves so that we might share in the experience of His holiness. As we grow in humility and holiness, we also grow in happiness because we learn that God is our best portion and that He exalts Himself in all that He is and in all that He does for His glory and our best good.

We may easily understand how we may delight in a God who loves us with an unbreakable covenant love as the names LORD, Jehovah, or Yahweh indicate, but the name used here for God describes His omnipotence. God is all-powerful; He possesses both the authority and the power to command compliance to all His holy will. He is the Almighty!

God is sovereign in all His ways, but one of our greatest difficulties, especially in time of trial, is in believing that He is both sovereign and good. In Zechariah 9:17, the Spirit of God appeals to us to consider "how great is his goodness." If God were not good, and if He did not "always do what is right" (cf. Gen. 18:25), then it would be impossible for us to take delight in His authority and power over us. But our great, omnipotent God is good and He "rejoices over them to do them good," as Jeremiah 32:41 says.

The world with all its wares seeks to allure us, just as it did Christian and Faithful in the town of Vanity Fair. How

---

3. Spurgeon, *The Metropolitan Tabernacle Pulpit,* 31:334.

was it that they showed so little interest in houses and lands and jobs and positions and honors and every other pleasure bought and sold in Vanity Fair? They showed little interest for the world because they cried out to God, "Turn our eyes away from worthless things."

We must fight the vanities of the world and worldliness, but we must also fight Satan.

Satan roams around like a roaring lion seeking to devour us with his deception and his trickery. And we are glad when the all-powerful arm of our Good Shepherd protects us against this great lion. But is it intense joy for you to know that this same God is all-powerful to carry out His will in your life to know Him and love Him above everything else? Does it bring lasting satisfaction to seek and savor the face of God? Is it pure pleasure for you to enjoy communion with Him? If enjoying your relationship with God brings greater happiness than anything else on earth, then it's clear that His omnipotent goodness and grace are at work in your life.

Can you really delight in a God whom you do not know? If earthly pleasure is your gold, can you enjoy communion with God? Can you lift up your face to God if you don't really trust Him? If we know and love God, if we repent of holding on too tightly to our earthly treasures, then God will be our gold. If we make the glories of God the source of our best meditation, then He will be our chief delight and we will lift up our face to Him. As we exercise faith in God, as we make use of the means of grace God Himself ordained, then we will be truly rich in our fellowship with God—rich beyond our wildest imagination—and we will have the best of the best. May we make use of every means of grace in order to grow in communion with God!

COME TO THE FEAST!

There is a feast of great despair
Which some men feel, when gathered there.
No sav'ry taste can they enjoy
When strength of will do they employ
To seat themselves without His grace
And so from them, He hides His face,
And so from them, He hides His face.

In those He's worked His sov'reign will,
Their hearts to conquer and to fill—
To see the glories of His face
And taste the goodness of His grace;
It spreads their wings in holy flight,
And comes to be their chief delight,
And comes to be their chief delight!

So now with these two set beside
At which table will you reside?
To cling with stealth to your resolve,
Or look to Him to guilt absolve?
To starve to death on self and sin,
Or Christ's great feast to enter in,
Or Christ's great feast to enter in?

Then lay your treasure in the dust;
Receive from Him what cannot rust!
And fix your gaze on Him, behold,
Then He will be your finest gold!
Oh plead with Him who freely gives,
Then in His riches you will live,
Then in His riches you will live![4]

---

4. Written by Murray Brett upon preaching a Communion

DISCUSS THE ISSUES

1. List each means of grace in Job 22:21–26 and the result of using each in the way God prescribes. Can there be any delight in an unknown God? Describe what it's like to "lay up God's word in your heart."

2. Is it possible to turn away from sin without turning towards God? Why or why not? What worldly pleasures and treasures tend to ensnare you the most?

3. If one of your best friends comes to you for counsel because he is out of fellowship with God and doesn't seem to understand why he can't restore that fellowship, what three questions would you ask to help your friend discover where his spiritual life has gone awry? Assuming your friend has been humbled sufficiently by God to receive your counsel, what steps will you encourage your friend to take tomorrow and the next day and the day after that in order to find God to be his greatest gold?

SOLVE THE SCENARIO

When Jay was in his early thirties, his business boomed year after year, so much so that he was able to turn the day-to-day operations over to his best friend and devote half his income and half his time to supporting church planting in Romania. It was a dream come true for him. When he was thirty-seven, Jay's home church asked him to serve as an

---

Meditation on 1 Corinthians 5:7–8 April 30, 2006, entitled "Come to the Feast." The last verse was written in preparation for a Communion Meditation on Job 22:21–26 entitled, "Lay All Your Gold in the Dust." Meter 8.8.8.8.8.8

elder. Though shouldering the burden of ministry with his fellow elders was a great labor of love, it became one of the most fulfilling parts of Jay's life. During his tenure, the church experienced unusual growth both spiritually and numerically. God seemed to be blessing Jay and using his life and ministry for great good.

Then Jay turned forty and he experienced something of "a mid-life crisis." For months he struggled to muster any desire at all for devotional reading of Scripture and personal prayer. After four months of spiritual drought, Jay became mentally, physically, and emotionally exhausted. He retreated to his study at home with little desire to do anything but sit in his big leather chair staring out the window. After two days of asking not to be disturbed, Jay's wife, Lynn, wisely called their dear old friend John. In his early eighties, but still very spry, John was everyone's dearest old friend. He was pastor emeritus of their church and well loved and respected by both young and old of their church and community. Others said of John that it was hard to tell the difference between what he was by nature and what he had become by grace because he loved people, all people, so deeply and so steadily. Finding pleasure in caring for people and doing fellow sinners good was what John did best.

When Lynn called, John came right away. When John entered Jay's study, Jay smiled slightly. John put his left hand on Jay's shoulder, gazed deeply and graciously into his eyes, took his right hand into his own, and squeezed warmly. For the first three days, neither Jay nor John said anything at all. Finally Jay spoke softly and told John his story. After telling his story, Jay became quiet and looked at John searchingly. When John spoke, Jay seemed puzzled but not disappointed. John quoted, "'No one can deny his deep distaste sometimes for spiritual duties and spiritual exercises; for secret prayer, for secret meditation, for secret self-examination, and for secret communion with God. And what is the source of all our spiritual distaste, but distaste, dislike, weariness, aversion, and almost enmity of God Himself?"[5] John, I want to encourage you to take the next three days to read the Scriptures devotionally and pray to discover your remaining hostility towards God and your disapproval of His ways. Especially take the second table of the law and use it to discover your lack of love for your neighbors and your lack of communion with them and therein also seek to discover your lack of love for God and your lack of communion with Him. I'll be back in three days and we'll talk about your discoveries."

After three days, what do you suppose John and Jay's conversation will be like?

SIT AT THE FEET OF CHRIST-CENTERED, EXPERIENTIAL TEACHERS

"A Rich Feast Prepared for Hungry Souls," sermon 7 in volume 10 of *The Works of Thomas Boston,* by Thomas Boston (*Level:* Intermediate)

Meditations and Discourses: Concerning the Glory of Christ in His Person, Office and Grace, in volume 1 of *The Works of John Owen,* by John Owen (*Level:* Intermediate to Difficult)

"The Grace and Duty of Being Spiritually Minded," in volume 7 of *The Works of John Owen,* by John Owen (*Level:* Intermediate to Difficult)

---

5. Alexander Whyte, "The Enmity that is in Me to God," in *Bunyan's Characters, 4th Series* (Rio, Wisconsin: Ages Software, 2006), 97.

Worship: The Ultimate Priority, by John MacArthur Jr. (*Level:* Basic)

Whatever Happened to Worship, by A. W. Tozer (*Level:* Basic)

"The Eternal Feast," in *Letters on Spiritual Subjects,* by Anne Dutton (*Level:* Basic) http://www.gracegems.org/Dutton/feast.htm

"Worship, The Feast of Christian Hedonism," by John Piper, (*Level:* Basic) www.desiringgod.org/ResourceLibrary/Sermons/ByDate/1983/406_Worship_The_Feast_of_Christian_Hedonism/

God is the Gospel: Meditations on God's Love as the Gift of Himself, by John Piper (*Level:* Basic)

Desiring God, by John Piper (*Level:* Basic)

When I Don't Desire God, by John Piper (*Level:* Basic)

The Pleasures of God: Meditations on God's Delight in Being God, by John Piper (*Level:* Basic to Intermediate)

"The Crown and Glory of the Christian Life, Or, Holiness, the Only Way to Happiness," by Thomas Brooks (*Level:* Intermediate) http://www.gracegems.org/Brooks/crown_and_glory_of_christianity.htm

"The Puritan Approach to Worship," chapter 15 in *The Quest for Godliness: The Puritan Vision of the Christian Life,* by J. I. Packer (*Level:* Intermediate)

2 Timothy 2:15

Study to shew thyself approved unto God, a workman that needeth not to be ashamed, rightly dividing the word of truth.

How to Make the Best Use of this Book

PERSONALLY AND IN SMALL GROUPS FOR THE
GLORY OF CHRIST, THE EQUIPPING OF THE
CHURCH, AND THE PROGRESS OF THE GOSPEL

ULTIMATE GOAL: We desire to keep our chief end, *to glorify and enjoy God forever,* at the forefront of this study, the whole of our lives, and the life of the church.

HOLISTIC DESIGN: Sacred Scripture is aimed at the whole person: mind, heart, and will. In Romans 6:17, Paul says that he gives thanks that the Roman Christians became obedient (involving the will), from the heart (engaging the affections), to that form of teaching (informing the mind) to which they were given over (by the power of the Holy Spirit). Second Timothy 3:16–17 adds that Scripture is inspired by God and profitable for teaching (to gain understanding and wisdom), reproof and correction (to shape godly character), and training in righteousness (to equip with skills for living). To profit spiritually from this book, we encourage you to:

- read and think carefully so that you may know, understand, internalize, apply, and express the truth of Scripture in order to pass the faith along to others and defend it against the error of unprincipled men;

- nurture life change so that your life will be renewed in the image of God;

- shape your values so that holy affections might be raised to heights consistent with the splendor and majesty of our great, Triune God;

- train in skills for life and ministry so that you might fulfill your calling in this world to make disciples.

THE CHURCH AS FAMILY: Christ died to build a church against which the gates of hell shall not prevail (Matt. 16:18). The institution created by God to put His glory on display in the world is His church (Eph. 3:20–21). In order to serve God best, we must grow in the experience of grace as individuals and as families without becoming isolated individualists or isolated families. The conduct of the church as a family is the pillar and support of the truth (1 Tim. 3:15–16). The visible love and unity of the church is instrumental in the progress of the gospel (John 17:20–23). God commands each member to be involved in intentional discipleship in the context of the local church (Matt. 28:19–20; Col. 1:28–29; Heb. 10:24-25; 13:17). Ezra's practice may serve well as a model for the relationship between personal study and our corporate involvement and responsibility in the life of the local church. Ezra prepared his heart to seek the law of the Lord, to put into practice, and to teach its statutes in the covenant community (Ezra 7:10).

GROUP STUDY: You may consider several options for using this book in a group setting. You may read a chapter prior to gathering for the discussion. In this case, allow for an hour to an hour and a half for a thorough discussion: 30–45 minutes to discuss the questions and an additional 30–45 minutes to discuss the scenario. You may prefer to read the chapter aloud on the evening of the group study in which case we recommend two separate sessions allotted for a single chapter. The full-length chapters may take 15–20 minutes to read aloud and the meditations from 10–15 minutes. During the first session in which the chapter is read aloud, discuss the questions; then at the next session, discuss the scenario.

FACILITATING THE DISCUSSION: We highly encourage an able and faithful teacher or mentor to lead the discussions. In order to facilitate a good discussion, the leader should pray for each participant, read the material carefully, and think through the discussion questions and scenario ahead of time. Then the leader should seek to be as warm and pastoral as possible with each person who participates in the group study. Seek to caringly inform the mind and conscience, engage the will, and inflame the heart for the sake of the glory and enjoyment of God.

SIT AT THE FEET OF CHRIST-CENTERED, EXPERIENTIAL TEACHERS: At the end of each chapter, we've provided references and links to articles, sermons, chapters of books, complete books, and audio files to complement the subject the chapter addressed. Our desire is to promote lifelong learning from worthy authors and speakers. We have only a limited time to read, listen, think, and pray, and we should seek to use the very best literature available. We encourage you towards Christ-centered teachers because the finished work of Christ is the only basis upon which we relate to God. Be careful to follow only those who set forth Christ in unambiguous terms as our only mediator. In our day, there's no end to "God-talk" and spirituality, but such talk often lacks the Person and work of Christ set forth clearly for needy sinners. We also lean towards experiential teachers because we truly believe that "experience is the food of all grace," as John Owen says in his third volume on the work of the Holy Spirit. We would discourage you from reading or listening to anyone who would aim merely to make you more knowledgeable, which a former generation called "speculative knowledge." This kind of knowledge puffs us up with pride. Instead, read and listen to those who encourage you towards "experiential knowledge," the kind of knowledge that humbles us before God and man and causes us to grow in love, trust, submission, self-denial, obedience, and community.